The Courage to Be Yourself

How to Be a Powerful, Confident, Successful Woman

Njideka N. Olatunde ND, MSW, PhD

The Courage to Be Yourself
Njideka N. Olatunde, ND, MSW, PhD

Be Empowered, LLC
Post Office Box 26132
Washington, District of Columbia 20001
www.thefeminatefactor.com
(702) 723-8104

Printed in the United States of America
First Edition, April, 2011

ISBN: 13 978-0-615-45793-2

Cover Designed by Izhar ul Haq
www.hcdesignhouse.com

DEDICATION

This book is dedicated to all women who are ready to pursue their dreams and passions that live in your heart and begin the journey to take back control of your life and let the little girl inside come out and play!

Acknowledgments

There are so many people I give thanks to for the creation of this book. Let me begin with my mentors who have held my hand and guided me in recreating my life so I can share my growth and development with you.

Johnny *"The Transition Man"* Campbell, professional speaker, my first mentor who helped me become the professional speaker I always wanted to be. He also introduced me to the world of internet technology that has opened many doors for me.

Heatherr Jumah, creator of Success Chicks CEO is not only my mentor but a friend and sister who has guided and supported me in recreating my life passion and vision that I have created in The Feminate Factor as my gift to women worldwide. She has been my rock of encouragement that is real blessing in my life.

A big thank you, to my book cover designer, Izhar ul Haq owner of hcdesignhouse. He is talented, professional, and most of all understanding with a willingness to please. Through all the cover revisions his patience's I am so humbly thankful and appreciative.

I am so thankful to my family who have lived and shared in this life journey with me and have been my inspiration every step of the way. Shabaka, my soul mate and best friend; Jah Richie, my brother; Ronald my son and Ronia my granddaughter. I am thankful and truly blessed you are in my life.

You can not write a book and not give thanks to you the reader, who I am humbly thankful for your appreciation, encouragement and support in me and my work. It is because of you that I share the message in this book.

Introductions

I wrote this book to show you how to tap into the power you have inside to begin to renew yourself so you can become the woman you are created to be..... bold, confident, powerful, beautiful, happy and successful. In writing this book I wanted it to be an extension of me. I want you feel that I am your friend who is holding your hand as we travel together along this path in making the lifestyle changes needed to take back control of your life. As you read this book I want you to hold this thought..... Imagine a day where you can be in the midst of chaos but maintain a clear head with a sense of balance and focus having your feet firmly planted on the ground and you are able to smile and say *"I am in perfect peace"*. This is the power that you have hidden inside of you. This is a gift that most women have and never learned how to use it.

The lack of perfect peace has held most women in bondage from being able to live the life of their dreams and passions. When you do not know peace you can not have courage. Discovering how to use this gift has given birth to this book, *The Courage to Be Yourself: How to Be a Powerful, Confident, Successful Woman.*

The basic premise behind this book is that any woman, no matter what her present circumstances or situation she has this gift, which gives her the power to can change her life for the better. Your happiness does not depend on what others say, how they act or think. Your happiness begins with being at peace with yourself.

When you understand your ability to use this hidden power with the thoughts and actions you take, you are on the road to defining the woman you want to become. This is the key that determines and defines who you are. It was not until I realized this fact that my life began to change. I saw that by changing my attitude toward me and my environment, the hidden gift of peace began to manifest. With this new awareness in my life I gained the courage to become the one who is the CIC (Chief In Charge) of my life.

As you read through the chapters in this book, I think you will find that you are not powerless in changing your circumstances or lifestyle realities and that no situation is unalterable. There is a great spiritual and universal force within every woman that is laying dormant ready to be called upon and used. There is a whole new world waiting for you. Start today to discover and experience your inner gift so you can pass it on.......

If women are perceived as potentials rather than problems, as possessing strengths instead of weaknesses, as unlimited rather that dull and unresponsive, then they thrive and grow to their capabilities

TABLE OF CONTENTS

Chapter One *Asking For What You Want*
Your Legitimate Needs ---10
Career or Job Which Is It--13
Robbing Pamela to Pay Patricia--23

Chapter Two *Is That Me in the Mirror*
Building Self Esteem--31
Define Yourself--33
Celebrate Strengths and Acknowledge Weaknesses----------36

Chapter Three *Face and Release Your Fears*
Building Confidence---44
Tap Into Your Talents--49
Dare to Dream and Go for It--53

Chapter Four *Stop the Worrying*
Put the Past to Rest--56
Get Out of Your Head--59
You Make Me Sick--63

Chapter Five *Accepting Who I Am*
Standing Up For Me---70
Defining Who I Am and Feeling Good About It-------------76
Become the New Chief in Charge-------------------------------------79

Chapter Six *It's a Family Affair*
Parenting Aint Easy---83
Mother Daughter Relationship--87
Mother Son Relationship---89
I'm a Grown Woman not Your Little Girl--------------------92
Hey Sister Hey Brother We Are Now Adults-------------------95

Chapter Seven *Relationship or Situation*
Letting Go Is So Hard to Do---98
Emotional Roller Coaster--100

Chapter Eight *Taking My Life Back*
It's Time to Change---116
Making Lifestyle Changes--------------------------------119
I'm In Love with Me---126

Resource Section *Empowering Women to Greatness*
Message of Inspiration--------------------------------------135
A Self Proclaimed Woman--------------------------------136
The ABC's of Loving Yourself --------------------------137
The Beauty of an Empowered Woman----------------142
A Tribute to the Empowered Woman-----------------143

Becoming the Women You Want To Be
Take Action Message---144
The Feminate Factor Edumercial----------------------------145

Meet the Author---148

Chapter One Asking For What You Want
Your Legitimate Needs

*Never allow a person to tell you No who doesn't have the power
to say Yes ~ Eleanor Roosevelt*

How hard is it to ask for what you want? This is probably the
number one problem most women have, asking for what they want.
To understand why asking is so hard, begins with a look at the
history of the women who created this difficulty that still exist in the
lives of many women today. During the 19th century, women had a
very specific and limited role in society. Their domain consisted of
the home and children, and they rarely strayed from this role.

The women's sphere was the home and the men's sphere was the
bread-winning job. These Victorian ideals were the norm for upper
and middle class families, and were instilled in the minds of women
for century's to come. The emerging values of nineteenth-century
America increasingly placed great emphasis upon a man's ability to
earn enough wages or salary to make his wife's labor unnecessary,
but this devaluation of women's labor left women searching for a
new understanding of themselves.

 In the desire of women, to find themselves lead to a new domestic
role of introducing religion and moral values to their families. While
economic development built a new America, women retained
responsibility for turning that growth and development into
civilization, known as the "cult of domesticity". The women of this
time, were middle class women, most of them married, and lived the
ideal of domesticity as the foundation for family life.

In the 20th century women began feeling a need for change and
equality. This was the time period of women wanting power and
prestige, which was under male control. Education was the focus
and was only available to upper class women. A carry over from the
previous century for woman of the middle and lower class was
religion and moral values, which was the education base for these
women.

What was interesting is the fact that these women were seen to be more religious than men and the strongest component of the congregations, despite the fact that the religious leaders of the day were all male.

Women made great strides in the 20th century such as engaging publicly in "male" activities, skirt lengths went up, hair was cut shorter than in the past, smoking in public, and worked toward attaining sexual freedom. Then there was the depression which dealt a shattering blow to women. This was a hard time for women who had gained so much and lost it to favoring men's' rights over women.

After the Depression, the traditional gender role changed, in fashion with women becoming more feminine. The country was now in a war and this effected women in a big way. Women were needed in the work force as a national necessity and a patriotic duty. These women were given new training and became very skilled and become better educated.

This was a time when many women were angry and resentful because they had found a degree of self-definition they had not previously known. At the end of the war women returned back into the home practicing an upscale version of the "cult of domesticity". This was the great era of consumerism. Women stayed home and worked to create a "haven" for men who work longer and harder to provide for them. The trade off was to keep women more firmly tied to the home raising children.

Then came the Viet Nam war, bring in the period of rebellion that created the civil rights and feminine movements. This was a defining time period for women because they were fighting for their rights and in the end social problems for women accelerated. This is when "its man's world" became very evident. Domestic and other violence against women increased and women in the professions began to realize advancements in their fields faced glass ceilings. To add to the mix there was an economic rift between women of social classes.

Educated employed middle and upper class women saw women who stayed home as being too stupid to work. The final reality was women were not only under pressure to prove that they could be as successful as men in the workforce, but to keep the home fires tended and keep their appearance up, too, to remain attractive to men. Through it all women did make some visible progress they learned that they could step into leadership roles in the political arena.

You have just taken a stroll down women's history lane. Why did I take you on this journey to answer my question "why is it so hard for women to ask for what they want"? If you really look at the evolution of today's woman you still see the roots of yesterday's woman being played out in her life. No matter how educated, how professional, how accomplish she is, she is still living her life defined by others. Her pain is so deep that when she is faced with asking for what she really wants she sees the hurt, frustration, and disappointment of the women she is an extension of.

Take a moment and think about the last time you were in a situation and deep down inside you wanted to ask for what you wanted and you didn't. What stopped you from asking? The answer is always "FEAR" which means you need to

Feel Emotion And Relax

Chapter One Asking For What You Want
Career or Job Which Is It

I discovered I always have choices and sometimes it's only a choice of attitude ~ Judith M. Knowlton

Work is an important part of life and it is where we spend most of our day. The question is what do you have a career or a job? In today's work environment women face so many challenges. The beginning challenge begins with how much women value their self worth as it relates to skills, talents and abilities. These are all the things that are required and used in the work force. It is because of how women see themselves when considering a job verses a career it is a known fact that women aim lower, get paid less. The question to ask is why do women feel they are not worthy of higher salaries and rewarding job positions?

Research studies have found that women, when seeking employment willingly accept lower paying jobs rather than put themselves in a competitive pay scheme, which ends up with women creating their own glass ceiling. If you think about this for minute, there has to be a reason that is a contributing factor to women settling for less. It is a historical fact that that the social norms behind women's apparent aversion to accepting higher paying and challenging jobs are established well before a woman enters the workforce.

Let's take a stroll down memory lane and look at the seeds planted in our psyche as a little girl growing up. Boys, growing up, received more encouragement to be competitive, while girls were frequently encouraged to be more cooperative.

This leads to women making less money because they are more willing to take less competitive positions than their male counterparts, which leads to accepting lower-paying jobs. These are the positions labeled "female cluster" paying on the lower scale domestic, clerical support, and administrative-type occupations.

For the women who are not willing to settle for having a job may choose as a career to start their own business. Women are making great strides in the businesses they are creating. The reality is women still face many challenges as they enter the business world dominated by their male counterpart who make and change the rules.

Here's an example of low self worth mindset, even for woman business owner. In a recent study on women's value of themselves showed that both men and women will judge a woman who asks for a higher starting salary less favorably than a man with the same credentials asking for the same thing.

Men are rewarded for their outspokenness, while women are expected to be silent and go along with the program for the greater good. As a little girl the seed planted to be more cooperative is so deeply rooted and is being passed on from generation to generation. As a woman today looking at the job I have can I say truthfully this is what I really want to do? If you will be honest with yourself your answer is probably no. Then you have to ask the question why am I staying in this job I do not like?

Well, the number one reason most women stay in jobs they do not like is because of life issues. The job satisfies basic needs for everyday survival; specifically looking at the fact that you need the benefits that a job may provide which give justification to staying in the position.

Realistically this is an acceptable reason, but the real reason is based on fear. This fear stems from the work role and responsibilities as to what you can and cannot contribute in the position you hold. Most of the times you may have come to a point where you no longer like your job or you've outgrown the job, but because you don't feel that you can do anything else, you will stay in that job. By staying in the job, you create a fear of I can't do any better than what you have.

Here are a few of the reasons why women they can not do any better and stay in jobs they do not like based on self induced fear. The number one reason is for whatever benefits are being provided to them, and number two is because they fear not being able to get a better job or a better paying job. This is a fear based on the feeling of not having the skills and talents to do anything other than what they already know how to do. So a lot of times women get comfortable and when they get comfortable, they do not move. By not moving, it causes them to stay in a position that they don't like doing day in and day out and they will not do anything else to move forward.

One of the things I would suggest in helping women to see their jobs in a different light, is to give meaning to your job or career. To give meaning begins when you realize that you have talents, skills and abilities that are worthy of the work you do and the position you hold. What this means is you have a valuable asset that your job needs and what you do and know can improve productivity and performance, which gives meaning to you and your job.

Utilizing your skills and talents to meet a missing need in your specific position, that only you can do is what can bring about the changes needed. When you can see yourself fulfilling this desire in your heart you need to say to yourself, *"I can do it, I feel bold enough, I feel confident enough, and I know I can help enhance my position or enhance the company I work for with my skills. I will bring it to the table by share it with my supervisor. I'm giving meaning to my job and I'm also giving meaning to myself"*.

In other words, when you can see your talents and skills as being valuable and you can turn them into something that can enhance your job with a meaning or purpose, you will improve the quality of your life. Just seeing value in what you and who you are can turn into a career opportunity that has your name on it.

When this happens, you have given meaning to a job you have created for yourself. It is no longer just a job it is your life passion being shared with the world. All it takes is stepping out and taking action on your idea that can put you in a situation that can lead you to becoming self employed.

This is what women need to look at, as it relates, to giving meaning to the work you do. When you give meaning to your job through the contribution of your talents and skills, just think about what it will mean to the world as a whole.

Empowerment tip, give meaning to your job by looking at your skills, talents and abilities. Look at your past experiences, a hobby, or something you really like to do and see how you can turn it into something that is as meaningful as a job or a new career experience for yourself.

As women we need to look at why we choose to accept whatever is asked of us in our jobs before we can give it meaning. For most women it is hard to not accept whatever is asked of us because we don't feel we have the right or the ability to speak up for ourselves. We are afraid to say yes or no, ask if someone else can do it, or can it be done at another time.

This goes back to that deep seated root as a little girl to just be cooperative. This trend of thought has instilled a fear in women that says you do not have the right to speak up for yourself, when it relates to being imposed upon by someone else to get something done. When this happens it creates what we see today as health problems, stress, and burnout.

Anything that's related to work overload, work frustrations or work stress is the result of women choosing not to say what they feel and thin. Instead women choose to accept whatever is asked of them with no questions asked. This means women do not question anything they just accept.

Sometimes it's important to ask and learn how to say the word "*why*" to every request that does not make sense to you. This is the only way you can be in control of what is asked of you. When you have the ability to reply to a request by saying, you can do it or you can not do it you begin to feel good about your response.

Remember the reason why women constantly accept whatever is asked of them, as I've said before, is related to self imposed fear of rejection. It is the fear that keeps us in the position of not feeling we have the right to speak up for ourselves. When we choose to accept the fear and it keeps us from being able to say exactly what and how we feel.

It does not matter what job assignment or career we have, it is very important that we maintain a sense of personal value and worth. One of the ways that we can give value to ourselves in our job assignments or career is first and foremost to ask each and every day " *what contribution did I make in my job today that made me feel good*"? *What did I do today that I can say I really feel good about my accomplishments?* The next thing that we need to do to get value is to give value to someone else that assists us in getting something done.

Learning how to say "Thank You" is one of the highest qualities in terms of validating yourself as well as validating someone else. This is a value that will always come back to you. When you can say thank you to somebody it also sends thanks back to you. In giving value, feel good about everything that you do no matter how bad the situation may seem in the day-to-day task. Focus on finding something that is good about your job. Find something that is good about an interaction you had on the job and validate that as being something good you did.

Take the time to feel good about who you are, what you can do and have done. I think it's really important for women to really feel good about the work that they do every day.

Before you leave your place of employment, as you are packing up to leave, take some time to reflect on the day. What was the one good thing that happened today for you on the job?

Close out your day leaving with the thought of what was good that happened on the job for you today. This is how to validate yourself so you will not take home anything negative that is connected to you and your job experience for the day.

This get's you in the habit of doing an end of the day " job mind cleansing", so each day you can end your work day thinking about what good happened to you. This is how you validate yourself and your work experience for the day. Validation builds self esteem which is needed to give you the power needed to move forward. If a career change or promotion is needed self validation is how you motivate yourself to take action. You will have a mental diary of your accomplishments that gives value to what it is you do and can contribute to your job or career.

Women have achieved many great accomplishments toward equality in the workforce and leadership. These achievements have been obtained at a high cost. Women are increasingly in touch the challenges inherent in owning and operating small, large, home-based or sole-proprietorship businesses. The question that keeps coming up is, what's keeping women from succeeding to the extent that men do in business? The answer lies in the fact that men define the rules of the game. So what are women doing to change the rules?

Women are seeing the need to imitate men when in leadership positions? In a quote by Gloria Steinem, *"Some of us are becoming the men we wanted to marry."* Women usually imitate men in leadership positions because they feel that's the only way they can be seen as being in control. When women realize that being in a leadership position and being a leader does not necessarily mean that you have to act like a male figure to lead..

This is a major problem in how women define what a leader is. Margaret Thatcher is quoted as saying: *"If you want something said, ask a man, if you want something done, ask a woman."* For women who object to such a statement and sit out to prove it wrong they are the ones who take on the leadership style and characteristics of their male counterpart.

When we look at leadership, a leader is defined as being a male figurehead? Dos this mean a leader is defined as someone who has all of the qualities and characteristics associated with a man being masculine, forceful and powerful from a male perspective? Is this how women define and see as being a leader? If this is the case it oftentimes puts women in the situation of imitating the male figure in their role as a leader.

To be in a leadership role does not necessarily mean that a woman has to imitate the leadership style, characteristics or qualities of her male counterpart. It is the inner power of her feminine energy that connects with her masculine energy that radiates the true leader she can be.

A woman can be a leader and not be a carbon copy of her male counterpart when she realizes that inside her is the power and the ability to lead. To be a leader begins with being in oneness with self. By having a knowing that this is a quality that all women have inside of them waiting to be used and shared with the world.

A woman's connection with her oneness is what allows her to be an innovative leader who is original. When she exhibits her leadership skills she knows how to challenge the status quo with workable solutions. When she leads and allows her feminine side to be her guide she is able to connect with people. She has the leadership power that inspires and motivates.

A woman in leadership also has the ability to build trust needed for cooperation and achieving "win-win" outcomes. When she is utilizing her leadership power from a feminine perspective she see things long range, keeping her eyes on the horizon using her knowledge, talent and skills to organize. As we look at the leadership power of a woman, why would a woman want to imitate her male counterpart?

The one thing that a woman leader needs to know that will definitely make her different and make her not be a male leader carbon copy, is that she knows how to create things which are a reflection of her purpose and passion. When a woman can come to the frontline not being a reflection of what Madison Avenue says and not be a reflection of what mainstream society says is the way you do things, is a woman who is a natural leader from a feminine perspective.

Taping into your feminine energy as a leader, is the only way for a woman to not be a carbon copy of her male counterpart. A male leader uses his masculine energy, which is forceful and physical. A female leader is inspiring, innovative, and creative in recognizing how to pull out the best in others to get the job done. This is what makes and defines a great and powerful leader.

Success is something everyone wants. Success on the job and in your career is a constant struggle that often holds women back. Some of the things that hold women back from being a success in the workforce is being humiliated every day by people who do not feel good about themselves. Another thing is never being acknowledged when you do something that makes a difference in the workplace, is a big success crusher. These are the things that are bound to hold anyone back from being successful.

When you are faced with all this negative energy and are bombarded day in and day with every thing that's wrong and bad, there's no room for you to feel successful about anything as it relates to your job or career.

Let's look at some of the things that block us from being successful, such as a supervisor, who may not be a person who's encouraging, so this would dampen a feeling of being successful.

We could be given assignments just because it's something that has to be done, but we may not have the skills or the ability to do it. This can hold us back. We can be placed in a position because of downsizing or layoffs that put us into a situation that we just don't like doing it or we're not really interested in doing it. If this is the case, how can you feel successful?

Looking at these examples shows just a few of the things in the workplace that hold us back from being or feeling successful. When things do not push us forward, do not connect with us or give us value and recognition, so we can feel positive about our contribution in the work we do we can not be or feel successful. This is something that will always hold you back.

Empowerment tip, you can use to release the barriers that may be holding you back from being successful, recognizing your abilities. You need to begin by looking at what capabilities you have; evaluate and access your skills; You need to ask yourself what contribution can you make and what contributions are you willing to make; Are you committed; Do you have the commitment to what you're being asked to do; Do you believe in what you're being asked to do?

When you can answer these questions you're on the road to achieving the success you desire. You will know you have the answers when what is being asked of you makes you feel good. When you can connect with the request based on trust, integrity, accomplishment, creativity, freedom, and flexibility to deliver in a way that makes you feel valuable, you will have broken the barriers that have held you back from being a success in the workforce.

When your connection is based on how you feel and your qualifications are based on the skills you have to offer, you hold the key to your success. Women the time is now for you to take the steps you need to put it all together to create the success in your life and the many lives of future generations.

NOTES

Chapter One Asking For What You Want
Robbing Pamela to Pay Patricia

The only problems that money can solve are money
problems ~ Mignon McLaughlin,

The major concern for many women is not having enough money to pay the bills. This is a serious problem faced by many women each and every day. The question we ask is why are so many women struggling to make ends meet? In a study by the National Center for Women and Retirement Research (NCWRR) it shows a direct correlation between a woman's personality characteristics and her financial habits. Assertiveness, openness to change, and an optimistic outlook are the qualities that tend to lead to smart money choices.

Author, and TV host Suze Orman believes our problems with money are a manifestations of problems in our life and relationships. Work on the money issues and many of the other problems will take care of themselves; or, work on the other problems and the money problems will take care of themselves. For many women, money is an emotionally charged issue. It may represent power, love, or control, especially in relationships. Our beliefs about money and our emotional attachments to it strongly influence the way we spend and handle money.

So many women are struggling to make ends meet because of spending habits for a particular reason or result. The money situations we face today are not really a result of what we have done, it's about living in an economy that is not friendly or supportive of women.

This economic realty for women is about constant changes as it relates to knowing how to financially put the pieces together so we are able to make ends meet. A woman, in today's economic picture has to stretch everything to survive. Women are masters in utilizing the few resources available to increase their cashflow. The real truth is women have so few financial resources to work with to make ends meet and this is a big financial struggle with a heavy price to pay.

This means women have a smaller amount of capital available to meet all of their needs. Forget about the wants. This is where the struggle begins, because paying debts that are out of control because of more bills than money coming each month. Looking at all the major expenses, most women have to deal with such as shelter, transportation, childcare, food, clothing and education is an inescapable financial burden. All these expenses are needs and are astronomically high in cost. This leaves no room to include anything related to social or fun activities. A result of having such a small amount of resources to cover all of these expenses is a struggle that women face on a daily basis to make ends meet.

For the many women who are able to ride the economic rollercoaster, I salute you. You have learned how to master the art of robbing Pamela to pay Patricia by stretching your pennies and turning them into dollars. When you know how to take control of the little that you do have and can turn it into dollars is the key that opens the door to make ends meet. This is the one major life lesson that women need to study and learn how to do.

Be real with yourself and take a serious look at your economic picture focusing your attention on and what is the real cause of your personal money struggle as it relates to meeting your financial expenses.

Empowerment tip, to stop struggling to make ends meet. Take some time to pull back, regroup and seriously look at your spending habits, patterns and belief systems. It's about prioritizing. When I say prioritizing, it's looking at what are the basic necessities that have to be met? These are the things you actually must have. They are your needs not your wants. We know we need shelter, clothing, and food. These three things are the major things that we know we have to have, so look at these needs, as it relates to the dollar amount you need and what you will need to do to getting it and maintain that amount coming in each and every month.

We need to ask ourselves, what is the amount I can put aside each pay period to cover this expense so I can make sure these bills get paid on time every month? You may need to look at learning how to use your talents and skills to create an additional stream of income. This is known as *"the creating money experience"*. Did you know that you can create your own money? Money can be created because it begins with an idea and the idea is nourished with energy, which creates money .

If you want to stop struggling financially you need money. To have money begins with learning how to make money as an additional source of income to your pay check. You also need to know some money management and budgeting strategies, which will also stop the money struggling. Some other possibilities to consider in stopping the cash drain is to look at the things you no longer are using, sell them to put more cash into your coffers.

Empowerment tip, to stop the hemorrhaging to seal the wound you will need to be open to change, making adjustments and being creative. The struggle can only stop when you begin to act and think outside of the box. To thinking outside the box look at, Do I have a skill I can trade for some services I need? Can I barter? Can I negotiate on pricing for a service and products I want to purchase? Take some time and put together your own "*creating money experience*" list. Make it a family affair and see what you come up with.

Understand this reality, you are on the front line in an economic war that has you struggling each and every day to make ends meet. What will it take for you to win the war? The answer is to look at how you can be as creative as you possibly know how. One of the things that I would suggest you do is to do a little research on looking into some of the things that your fore parents did to survive during times of economic hardship. You will be surprise at the economic tips you find that can become a financial life raft for you.

The research, I am suggesting is look at some of the family strategies of those family members who had and used a plan that got them through the times of the Depression or who went through the early part of what was known as the Recession. Talk to the elders in your family or community and listen to their wisdom about the things they did in terms of being able to make ends meet.

Learn the techniques and see how you can incorporate what you learn as it relates to the economic times of today in the 21st Century. Your goal is to take what you can use to develop your system using some of the same strategies to improve your daily, monthly or weekly cash flow if that's what's needed. Always remember *"there is nothing new under the sun only recycled experiences and lessons"*.

To achieve the goal of stop struggling to make ends meet begins with being creative and thinking innovatively with ideas and concepts that you may have never thought of before. Let your focus begin with being able to stretch what little dollars you have in to multiple streams of incomes affectionately known as "cashflow".

It is casflow that ends all money struggles. To have cashflow means knowing how to look at ways you can multiply dollars not add dollars. When you multiply dollars you are stretching your dollars so the struggle begins to decrease instead of increase. To stop the struggle of robbing Pamela to Pay Patricia begin with being creative and innovative with your ideas that will improve your cash flow whether you need it weekly or monthly.

Here is an insightful message of what has helped me. If you aren't where you should be money wise, examine what drives you emotionally when it comes to money and try to figure out the psychological stumbling blocks that keep you from becoming financially free. Here are ten of the most important things women can do for themselves and their financial future:

1. Don't rely on someone else, like a husband, boyfriend or significant other, for your financial security. Educate yourself about money management and investing.

2. Develop a money action plan - it's key to financial success.

3. Don't use money to make yourself feel good. That type of high serves no purpose. Instead, do things that promote self-respect and creativity so you don't have to seek those feelings through spending money

4. Spend less than you earn - it's the secret to creating a cashflow

5. Get an education. People with college degrees or a skill make on average significantly more money than those who don't have degrees or certifications

6. Build an emergency fund. Without one, losing your job or incurring a large unexpected bill could force you to take on heavy credit card debt, and could put you into a financial hole that will be difficult if not impossible to dig your way out of.

7. Be involved in the day-to-day management of your family's finances, and talk about money with your spouse, significant other and children

8. Don't take on your partner's or spouse's debt. Wait until you're both out of debt before doing financial joint ventures.

9. Don't let the fear of losing money, fear of failure, or fear of the unknown stop you from investing.

10. Learn from your money mistakes. Don't let them hold you in shackles.

Your financial freedom is dependent on your attitudes and beliefs about money and your willingness to take back control of your financial destiny is in your own hands.

On the serious side of the money struggles, as it relates to women begins with our spending habits. It is always mention that women usually spend beyond their means and the question asked is why?

Some of the reasons why women spend beyond their means really relates to being frustrated or having to always pay bills and not having enough to do at least one thing that feels good to you. This means for many women, who are spending beyond their means use spending as a form of therapy. Spending is often seen as a self therapy session for women. This type of therapy is a way for women to say "this is how I'm able to release the daily stress so I can feel good about myself".

The spending reality for women is "I did something good for myself today". The question that needs an answer is how did I do something good for me? The answer is *I spent some money today*. What did I do? Your answer will be *I spent some money today on something that I know I can't afford, but when I was in the store looking at it, it sure made me feel good. When it made me feel good, I bought it.* This is the reality it did not matter whether you could afford it because you'll deal with that matter later. Your rational is *"I refuse to deal with it now because what is important right now is that I feel good"*.

This is the reality behind why so many women usually spend beyond their means, to make themselves feel good. Life sends so many experiences that affect us emotionally and can become a trigger in spending beyond our means. When we're angry or upset about something to ease the pain we spend money.

Pretending to have and comparing yourself with others by keeping up with your next door neighbor, keeping up with the Joneses, and keeping up with what Madison Avenue dictates can be a contributor in your spending beyond your means. All these things are emotional reasons used to spend money we do not have readily available to spend. When you satisfy your emotional urge you are creating an unnecessary financial struggle that can take a life time to recover from.

Spending as we all know, is a pleasurable feeling. How about turning your spending into something that can be beneficial and improve your financial situation?

I think this could be good replacement for the spending beyond your means self therapy. Women you can turn spending into something that can be beneficial and improve your financial situation when you take the time, as I always say, to become financially literate. When you are financially literate, you understand the total economic picture about financial value versus things that have no financial value. Being financially literate is about knowing how to make your money work for you, rather than you always working for money.

When you understand what assets and liabilities are, you begin to create a beneficial and improved financial situation. What you need to know about an asset and a liability, as it relates to spending money is when I spend am I spending on something that's going to make me money (an asset) versus something that's going to constantly keep taking money away from me (a liability). If you keep this in mind when you get that urge to satisfy that emotional spending urge think asset verse liability.

As women we need to learn about all the things we can do to improve our economic reality. This does not always necessarily mean that you need to get into investing. What you need is something of value that will make you money. This can be an idea. The question to ask is, how can I turn my idea into something that will make money for me? Take a minute and think about a hobby or something you like to do that others have asked you about and would like for you to do for them. This is how you turn an idea into making money for you. Then it becomes an asset. Or it can be something of value that you are no longer using. You can sell it? If you sell it, the thing that once was valuable, and you are no longer in need of it or using has now made you money ,which is an asset.

These are some food for thought concepts you can use to change your economic reality. Think about the concept shared and see how you can begin to turn an idea or something you have into a money making value versus something that's a money drainer. If we are ever going to win the economic war against women and turn things around financially we must begin by changing the way we spend money.

Our message to Madison Avenue and the powers that be needs to be our spending habits have changed. We will only spend money on things that will benefit and improve our financial situation. The bottom line is whatever we spend our money on from now on will be based on answering this question, **is *it something that will make money for me*.**

For all women interested in having the resources, resolve and intent to take back control of your financial destiny, this will not happen until you seriously start looking at the things that will make you money rather than things that make you spend money.

A woman who has no way of expressing herself and of realizing herself as a full human being has nothing else to turn to but the owning of material things ~
Enriqueta Longauex-Vasquez

Chapter Two Is That Me in the Mirror
Building Self Esteem

A strong, positive self-image is the best possible preparation for success ~ Joyce Brothers

Building Self Esteem is the most underrated ingredient for success and happiness in life. Your level of self-esteem influences not only the way you think about yourself, but also the manner in which you behave on a regular basis. Although the truth behind how we develop our level of self-esteem is surrounded by fact and fiction, it remains a fact that our self-esteem is an integral part of our lives. The world we live and work in is marked by unprecedented change and complexity. For many women, life begins to look like an uphill struggle to survive instead of a fun and exciting opportunity to grow, risk, and play fully in our relationships with others. The stresses, conflicts and frustrations we experience daily do not have to be our reality.

Reinventing ourselves, our relationships with others and our perception of the world is the result of a never ending commitment to our personal glory and the glory that exist in those around us. This becomes possible when we learning how to acknowledge and accept ourselves and others for we are as women growing and developing. This is the self esteem building key that opens the door for women to begin to view life and each other in an entirely different way. When we really "understand" the key to building self esteem in our lives and relationships new possibilities with life changing breakthroughs will always show up to lead and guide us in many totally different ways.

Having grown up with low self-esteem, I am able to see and relate to many issues from a personal and professional point of view. I understand and know the pain, frustration, and the cries for help. To have low self esteem is like being in jail cell. You are confined in a place where you can only do, think, be and live in accordance to the rules dictated by someone else. Take a moment to visualize exactly what that feels like. To have low self esteem affects the core essence of who you are as woman and human being. When you do not have self esteem, you always feel that something is missing in your life.

How can life ever be a fun, happy and a rewarding experience if you don't have self-confidence, know who you really are, what you want, or why you're here?

I have observed that healthy self-esteem rarely comes easily to any of us. Our childhoods, peer pressure, society's relentless demands and just plain stress prevents us from maintaining a healthy sense of self. How can you find balance? How do you stop the negativity in your head? How can you re-claim your life?

On my journey in building my self esteem I learned 10 essential skills that I have applied to my life. I invite you to try them out and hopefully they will help you in building your self esteem. The first instruction given was I must learn how to *be happy with myself* as I learn to incorporate these skills in my mind as a daily life practice:

1. Know Yourself

2. Love Yourself

3. Be True To Yourself.

4. Have a Personal Value System

5. Think for Yourself

6. Have an Open Mind

7. Have a Sense of Humor

8. Be Strong, Determined and Persistent

9. Have Acceptance with Understanding

Building Self Esteem is an ongoing process and journey. As, Oprah Winfrey has said: *"It doesn't matter who you are or where you come from. The ability to triumph begins with you. Always."*

Chapter Two Is That Me in the Mirror
Define Yourself

If I have to, I can do anything. I am strong, I am invincible,
I am Woman ~ Helen Reddy

How do you define yourself? When asked, who do you say you are? It's so easy to get your identity tangled up in your career, work roles or job titles. We seem to believe that we are what we do. We define ourselves solely in terms of the role or roles we play in life.

Women we are not things. It's so easy to use such labels to describe ourselves or define others. We say them so effortlessly and often we come to think of ourselves and others purely in one-dimensional terms. We all have a list of characteristics and behaviors that we use to define who we are. For successful women, these characteristics can be described by very positive words, such as: "intelligent," "committed," "results oriented," or "accomplished." Almost all of us have a few negative terms that are part of our self-definition. Common negative self-descriptions can be: "stubborn," "opinionated," or "I always have to be right."

One of the greatest challenges that we face, when we try to improve ourselves as leaders, partners, friends or family members is the challenge of changing the way we define ourselves. Our common reply is "That's just the way I am." The reality is, as long as we keep saying "That's just the way I am" to ourselves we increase the probabilities of "That's just the way I am always going to be." I believe we can all change our behavior. By definition, the only behaviors that we cannot changes are either shaped by genetic preconditions (we are born that way) or environmental factors (external forces that prohibit us from changing).

One of the hardest things in the world to do is define yourself. It is quite easy to define someone else, but to actually recall who you are is pretty difficult because basically most of us do not think very highly of ourselves. As women we use our emotions and emotions are contagious. How most women conduct themselves and what values we live by define our culture. The most important influence we have is ourselves.

We spend more time listening to our own self-talk than to anyone else. It is important that we make sure that the self talk we are listening to is in our best interest and worth hearing. Since emotions are contagious, the people in our lives can influence how we are feeling and sometimes will have more impact than we can withstand. Toxic personalities, for instance, tend to be strong and it's difficult to stand up to negativity for an extended period of time.

Somehow it's easier to be cynical, angry and bitter than it is to be cheerful, positive and upbeat, because there are plenty of reasons to be negative if that's what you choose. Pessimists are more often right (Murphy's Law!), but optimists accomplish more (ignore it and carry on!) Being around negative people can wear you down, exhaust you, and begin to subtly infiltrate your attitudes and feelings. This can be a big contributor in creating the negative definition that is defining who you are. When in a situation that has you looking at yourself and not liking who you see, means its time to surround yourself with the kind of people you are and want to have in your life.

Be more of who you are and you'll attract people like yourself. If you aren't optimistic, try it on for size it you just might like the fit. It's an emotional lesson you can learned.

Take a moment and answer these questions that may help you determine how your own self-definitions are propelling you to success or inhibiting you from positive change. Make two lists of the adjectives that you would use to define yourself: positive and negative. Review the words on each list:

* What are the positive words that can help you to feel successful?

* What are the negative words that are holding you back?

* Ask yourself, "Is there any genetic or environmental reason that I have demonstrated the behaviors on the negative side of my list?" If the answer is "no" there is hope.......you can get better.

Think about the words you use in defining yourself and others. We talk about the harmful impact the words we use when we define others in a negative way. What about the impact we often fail to consider when we define ourselves in a negative way? I ask the question how, do you define yourself. Think about this question and use this as your guide in answering the question, "Who am I?"

See if you can define yourself in terms of something besides your job or a certain group whose beliefs and members you identify with. Recognize that no label, however broad or descriptive can ever fully capture the unique, one-of-a-kind essence of you. I invite you to look inside and see that woman, called "YOU". Begin to see the unclaimed treasures that are waiting to be exposed when you give up the useless and meaningless label used to define the woman you are not. Define yourself today, the world is waiting to meet the real you.

Chapter Two Is That Me in the Mirror
Celebrate Strengths and Acknowledge Weaknesses

You may encounter many defeats, but you must not be defeated. In fact, it may be necessary to encounter the defeats, so you can know who you are, what you can rise from, how you can still come out of it ~ Maya Angelou

For most of us we are painfully aware of the weaknesses that hold us back and yet, surprisingly, we are unaware of our many strengths. It is so easy to focus on our weaknesses and ignoring our strengths. Every day 24/7 we are faced with the negativity of doom and glow that reflect weaknesses in our society and life in general. Failing to glorifying our strengths while up holding our weaknesses is unproductive. It is only when we learn to celebrate our strengths and acknowledge our weaknesses that we can realize our fullest potential.

To do this begins with choosing our friends carefully because through relationships our strengths and weaknesses are nurtured. The outcome is, we will grow for better or worse, depending on whom we spend our time with. In the big picture of our lives we all want to be powerful. By powerful, I don't mean ruling over others, but ruling over ourselves. We will never reach our dreams unless we first master ourselves? This is why understanding and managing our weaknesses is so important.

The first lesson, to remember is weakness means the absence of power. The question we have to ask is not "Do I want to overcome this weakness?" but "Do I want to be powerful or powerless?"

Weakness is nothing to be ashamed of; it is part of human nature. We are not dealing with a moral issue, but a practical one. That is, we want to know what works. What will help us reach our goals? It is not weakness but strength that will take us where we want to go. So it is very important that we identify our weaknesses so we can overcome or manage them.

We also have to realize that we will never overcome ALL our weaknesses, nor should we want to. For weaknesses are important. They help us to become a unique individual.

You see, it is not only the strengths of others that influence who we are, but also their weaknesses as well. We relate to the flaws inside ourselves as seen by others, as recognition that we are human and imperfect. As we open up and expose our weaknesses to friends, we develop intimacy that strengthens our relationship. In fact, weaknesses contribute to our greatest relationship, our love of life and self, which is who we see in the mirror.

You take your life in your own hands, and what happens?
A terrible thing: no one to blame ~.Erica Jong

The first step in overcoming any weakness is to become aware of it. So, how do we detect character flaws that are hiding in the background? A good way to start is by monitoring your negative emotions. Are we angry, vengeful, resentful, jealous, envious...? They all point to weaknesses that we can work on.

What we can do to acknowledge our weaknesses is to Change those traits. The important thing is not overcoming them, but to gain the strength in recognizing and doing what is needed to make the change and accept those traits you cannot change. Regularly reflect back on the ones you can't change, for what you can't change today, you may be able to change tomorrow. Embrace those you cannot change because this is what makes you unique. If everyone were perfect, everyone would be the same, and we would live in a dull world.

Use your weaknesses to develop compassion. Since others have to tolerate your faults, it is only fair that you tolerate theirs. Also use your flaws to learn new coping skills and strategies. In other words, use your weaknesses to find new strength.

Some examples of weakness to watch are:
1. Envy. If you envy (or admire) someone, that is useful information. It points to the person you would like to become. So make that your goal. You can even ask the person you admire how you can become more like them. They may not only be happy to help, but may develop into an important friend.

2. Anger and resentment. Here is useful advice from the late August Wilson, *"Confront the dark parts of yourself, and work to banish them with illumination and forgiveness. Your willingness to wrestle with your demons will cause your angels to sing. Use the pain as fuel, as a reminder of your strength."*

3. Ingratitude. Failure to be grateful for what we have prevents us from being happy, weakens relationships, and blocks more good from entering our lives. Live with a grateful heart and you will live a long, happy life.

4. Arrogant. People who think they know it all weaken themselves because they stop learning. They are also easily hurt by the criticism of others. The paradox is they become weak because of their fear of appearing weak.

5. Gullibility. To accept as true whatever one reads or hears without questioning the facts may leave one misinformed, ignorant, or open to manipulation by others.

6. Insecurity. To be uncomfortable with insecurity is to be uncomfortable with life, for insecurity is the nature of life. If you need to satisfy your hunger for security, rest with the assurance that although you cannot count on others or the world, you can always count on yourself. So, use your feelings of insecurity as a catalyst to develop self-reliance.

7. Failure. Failure is not possible unless one stops trying. Its cures are perseverance, patience, commitment, flexibility, creativity, and solution-oriented thinking. "*There is no failure except in no longer trying. There is no defeat except from within, no really insurmountable barrier save our own inherent weakness of purpose.*" Kin Hubbard

8. Boredom. Boredom is a lack of interest in doing anything. Its equivalent to feeling life isn't interesting. Whenever you are troubled with boredom, rather than asking yourself why you don't feel like doing anything, ask what you SHOULD be doing. Why? Because what you SHOULD be doing is what you really WANT to do.

Empowerment tip, the reason you don't see your weaknesses is not because you can not recognize them, it is because your subconscious mind creates a wall of resistance to camouflage your weaknesses as strengths.

The need to celebrate your strengths lays the foundation that allows you to be the woman you are created to be. It is our strengths that define our true essence and inner power. We all have strengths. You may not believe it but you have enormous power inside you that is often overlooked and neglected. I'm referring to the power of commitment. With it you can do the 'impossible' possible. As women we do not lack strength; we lack commitment. When you cultivate your desire to make a commitment, you will have a solid foundation for success.

In celebrating strength it is also important to recognize when you are weak. You need to know your weaknesses so you can manage your life because a sign of weakness is to be unaware of your faults and mistakenly believe you are strong. Oddly enough, these are real issue many woman faces that keeps them powerless. This is a crucial point in our growth and development because it is important that we recognize our inner power and stop failing to use it. This is where your strength to succeed comes from. The sad fact is a strong woman unaware of her strength is no more useful than a weak woman.

How can we make sure we are not overlooking our strengths? A good way to identify your personal strengths is to ask yourself a series of questions, such as the following:

Do I hunger for success?

Do I set goals and am I eager to take action to realize them?

Am I excited by life?

Am I curious?

Do I love adventure?

Do I live courageously?

Do I like to support others, lead others, or both?

Am I patient? Am I a risk taker?

Do I get along with others?

Do I look at the pros and cons before acting?

Can I depend on myself?

Do I encourage others and offer praise where it is due?

Do I respect and learn from others?

Do I see the potential in others and in myself?

Do I control my emotions or do I allow them to control me?

Do I balance work and recreation?

Do I look after my general well- being or do I neglect myself?

Am I organized?

Am I a visionary and see what others miss?

Do I have a positive outlook? Am I a peacemaker?

Do I empathize with others? Am I interested in what works and what doesn't?

Do I embrace change or do I prefer the status quo?

Do I love to learn and apply new things?

Am I a thinker, planner, and doer?

Do I always strive to do my best?

Am I gentle and kind?

Am I generous?

Am I understanding and accepting?

When celebrating your strength it is also important to be aware of your strengths' becoming your weaknesses. Self-confidence is good, but when we are too confident, we stop learning. When we are overly concerned about personal problems, we become blind to the problems of others. It is good to be prudent, but unless we are willing to take risks, we cannot go very far in life.

Decisiveness is strength, but guard against stubbornness; Striking while the iron is hot is a positive trait, but acting rashly can lead to a downfall

Self-discipline can lead you to expect too much of others

Thoroughness is good, but it can turn into perfectionism

It's good to be supportive, but not when you conform to every wish of others

If you are too patient, things may never get done

Diplomacy helps, but not when you allow others to take advantage of you

Self-starters sometimes have problems working harmoniously with others

Decisiveness is a strength, but not when you fail to consider other viewpoints

Determination is a strong point, unless one is headstrong, one-sided, and aggressive

Being a good speaker is an asset, unless one talks too much Enthusiasm is contagious, but enthusiastic people can come on too strong

Creativity and an active imagination make some visionaries and others unrealistic dreamers.

Here are some examples of strength:

1. Faith, trust, and confidence.

2. Excited by life.

3. Living Courageously. "Strength *does not come from winning. Your struggles develop your strength. When you go through hardship and decide not to surrender, that is strength."* Arnold Schwarzenegger

4. Getting along with others.

5. Self-discipline (self-leadership). Self-discipline is an essential ingredient of success, and, therefore, a major strength.

6. Follow-through. The greatest idea and the finest intention are utterly worthless unless we follow through.

7. Compassion. Compassion is love in action. The more of it we give away, the more of it comes back to us. Here's something to keep in mind; if we are not compassionate toward others, how can we be compassionate toward ourselves?

8. Responsibility. We all have challenges, when we accept responsibility; we realize that there is a universal power that helps those who help themselves. Sure, there are always excuses available if you are weak enough to use them, but wouldn't you rather be strong?

Remember this *"It is a wise woman who admits her weaknesses and celebrates her strength"*!

Inquiring minds want to know are you a wise woman?

Chapter Three Face and Release Your Fears
Building Confidence

Self-pity is our worst enemy and if we yield to it, we can never do anything wise in this world ~ Helen Keller

Self confidence is the difference between feeling unstoppable and feeling scared out of your wits. Your perception of yourself has an enormous impact on how others perceive you. Perception is a self imposed reality you have created of yourself. The more self confidence you have, the more likely it is you'll succeed.

From the quietly confident doctor whose advice we rely on, to the charismatic confidence of an inspiring speaker, self-confident people have qualities that everyone admires. Self-confidence is extremely important in almost every aspect of our lives, yet so many women struggle with finding it. Sadly, this can be a vicious circle: Women who lack self-confidence find it difficult to know happiness and success in their lives. The quality of a self-confident woman inspires confidence in others: their audience, their peers, their colleagues, their customers, their friends and their family. The ability to gain the confidence of others is one of the key ways in which a self-confident person finds happiness and success.

There is good news is if your self confidence is low you can learn how to build it up. The outcome in building your self confidence is well-worth the effort. Your level of self-confidence can show in many ways: your behavior, your body language, how you speak, what you say, and so on. Take a look at the list and see where you are as it relates to being self confident

Self Confident:
* Doing what you believe to be right, even if others mock or criticize you for it.

* Being willing to take risks and go the extra mile to achieve better things.

* Admitting your mistakes, and learning from them.

---

* Waiting for others to congratulate you on your accomplishments.

* Accepting compliments graciously. "Thanks, I really worked hard on that proposal. I'm pleased you appreciate my efforts."

Low Self Confidence:
* Governing your behavior based on what other people think.

* Staying in your comfort zone, fearing failure and so avoid taking risks.

* Working hard to cover up mistakes and hoping that you can fix the problem before anyone notices.

* Always speaking about what you have done as often as possible to as many people as possible.

* Dismissing compliments off handedly. "Oh that proposal as nothing really, anyone could have done it."

In looking at these examples, you can see how low self-confidence can be self-destructive, and it often manifests itself as negativity. Self-confident women are generally more positive they believe in themselves and their abilities, and they also believe in living life to the fullest.

What is Self Confidence?
There are two main things that contribute to self confidence, self efficacy and self esteem. We gain a sense of self-efficacy when we see ourselves (and others similar to ourselves) mastering skills and achieving goals that matter in those skill areas. This is the confidence if learned and worked on in a particular area, we'll succeed; and it's this type of confidence that helps women to accept difficult challenges, and persist in the face of setbacks. This overlaps with the idea of self-esteem, which in a more general sense relates to our ability to cope with what's going on in our lives, and that we have a right to be happy.

Partly, this comes from a feeling of being approved by the people around us and in our lives, which we may or may not be able to control.

—

45

However, it also comes from the sense that we are behaving victoriously, we're competent at what we do, and we can compete successfully in whatever we put our minds to do.

How do you Build Self Confidence?

In the process of building self confidence there's no quick fix, or 5-minute solution. The good news is that building self-confidence is readily achievable, as long as you have the focus and determination to see things through. What is so great and even better is that the things you'll do to build self-confidence will also build success and lead to happiness. The hidden jewel of building self confidence is your confidence will come from a real, solid achievement that No-One can take away from you! Here are a few steps you can take to begin the journey in building or strengthening your self confidence

* Look at what you've already achieved: Think about your present life and list the ten best things you've achieved in an "Achievement Log." Perhaps you scored high on important test or exam, played a key role in an important team project, produced the best sales figures in a period, did something that made a key difference in someone else's life, or present an idea that meant a lot for your business.

Write these accomplishments in a formatted document that you can look at and read daily. Make it a habit of spending a few minutes each week enjoying the success you've achieved!

* Think about your strengths: Next, take a look at who and where you are. Looking at your Achievement Log, and reflecting on your recent life, think about what your friends would consider being your strengths and weaknesses. From these, think about the opportunities and treats that are in store for you..

Make sure you enjoy a few minutes each day reflecting on your strengths!

* Think about what's important to you, and where you want to go: Begin by thinking about the things that are really important to you, and what you really want to achieve in your life.

46

Setting and developing an action plan is the key component in building real self-confidence. When you set and develop your action plan, begin the process needed by creating targets so you can measure your success in reaching your target goals. In set-up and developing an action plan let your emphasis be on exploiting your strengths, minimize your weaknesses, realize your opportunities, and control the threats and negativity you face.

Empowerment tip: Make sure you take small steps in reaching and keeping the target goals you have defined for yourself. Success and happiness is your reward and I want you to achieve it by taking no more than an hour a day to add your target goals until you complete the action plan. When the action plan is complete begin each day acknowledging your success in reaching your target goal.

* Start managing your mind: This is where the rubber hits the road in building and achieving self confidence, you need to manage your mind. Learn how to hear and listen to the defeat messages inside your head, known as <u>negative self-talk,</u> which can destroy your confidence. The saying, "*you are what you think*" becomes a real driving force in keeping your self confidence at its lowest level. If there has never been a time in your life when you need to be in control of what you think, it is right now.

When you are in control of your thoughts you have the magical power of accomplishment that is exclusively yours and no one can ever take it from you.

* Make a Commit to Success: Isn't this what, being self confident is all about. As women on the journey to make a difference in the lives of your communities and the world you need to make a clear and unequivocal promise to yourself that you are absolutely and totally committed to becoming strong, bold, fearless, powerful, and successful self confident woman who will do all in her power to achieve it.

47

As has been said building and strengthening self confidence is not an easy task. This is about making a life style change, its about letting go of old beliefs and habits, and it may be about letting go of friends and family who are not able to travel this journey with you. I know because I have gone through all of these experiences on my own personal journey to build my self confidence. Here are some things I did to keep me on the straight and narrow path, when you find doubts starting to surface write them down and mentally challenge them calmly and rationally. If they dissolve under scrutiny, that's great. However if they are based on genuine risks, remind yourself that you are getting ready to face a life lesson, meaning there is something you need to learn. Whatever life lesson you need to learn, move through it knowing that the letters in risk stand for **R**eleasing **I**nner **S**trength **K**nowingly (RISK).

One important key to success is self-confidence. An important key to self-confidence is preparation ~ Arthur Ashe

Chapter Three Face and Release Your Fears
Tap Into Your Talents

*We must believe that we are gifted for something, and that this thing, at whatever
cost, must be attained.* ~ Marie Curie

Every woman has a talent. "EVERY WOMAN"
Talents are different than skills, in that they tend to be innate rather than
learned. Once found, they can be nurtured and developed, but finding
them can be tricky. It's partly a process of self-observation and honesty.
The rest is learning and practice. Talents can come in many varieties.
They may be artistic or technical, mental or physical, inwardly or
outwardly directed. They need not be profitable, useful, or conventional,
but they will always be what makes and defines you. In the past hidden
talents have commonly been known as things you are great at but
nobody knows it, or things that you would immediately be great at if you
did them or being able to just skip beginner and progressing to
intermediate in an instant

Your hidden talents are the things you do that make you happy. What
you don't know it is this is not just about work, but about the quality of
your life. I've already written about the psychological evidence that
shows that when people do work or activities that make them feel good
and involve skills, either mental or physical, live happier lives. This is just
common sense, and it's probably nothing you haven't already heard
before. But I don't think many women actually take the next step and
give themselves the opportunity to discover all of their hidden talents.

If you take a pen and paper and write down a list of all the things you've
always thought you might enjoy or be good at, you'll be surprised at how
many of them you can test and give it a try within 7 days. With the help
of the internet, it's easy to find local classes, get how-to books,
recommendations, follow along with tutorials and find other people who
can answer your newbie questions. There is no real excuse to miss out
on finding your hidden talents. If the entry barrier for your hidden talent
is too high begin by offering to teach someone how you learned how to
do what you do at senior citizen or youth programs. You never know
who will see what you bring to the community as valuable asset and
resource.

There is always a way to make your hidden gift accessible. Consider sharing your work at community fairs to show how talented and skillful you are. If you enjoy what you do take the next step toward accomplishing this goal.

You might also worry that your real hidden talent is not on your list. It's so hidden that you've never even thought about it as something you might like to do. If you usually hate exercise, you might never expect that you'd love hiking, for example. But your hidden talents are never that random. You might hate exercise but love nature, so it makes sense that you'd enjoy relatively easy hikes. But you'd be hard-pressed to find a passionate hiker who hates exercise and is bored by natural beauty! Your hidden talents will always fit your personality or interests in some way. Instead of being hidden and random your talents are things to be discovered by accident. These are the things you love doing and make a lot of sense to you. You can find a good beginner's lesson on anything for free, online. This is an incredible privilege of living in the era of technology and the internet, which provides us with endless opportunities.

50 or 100 years ago, a farm girl in a small rural town who loved designing clothes may never have been able to learn more about it. Her small local library didn't have the books, she didn't know anyone who could teach her, she didn't know where to travel to buy materials or join classes. So she never had the opportunity to find the hidden talent that would make her happy. As for us, the barriers to entry are so low that there's no excuse not to give yourself that opportunity. Go online, Google the phrases 'designing clothes classes', 'designing clothes resources' or 'designing clothes lessons' and in 5 seconds you have more opportunity than that farm girl ever did to pursue a talent that could have been her life's calling. The free and instant access to answers, advice and learning materials on any topic is, in my mind, the universe's greatest gift to humanity.

How to Find Your Talent
First, figure out what are the benefits you are getting by NOT finding your own talent.

For example, are you really afraid to try something new because it might not work, so not letting your talents surface gives you an excuse to affirm not succeeding or do you just feel safer being able to blame your problems (boredom, lack of money, poor health) on someone or something else? Once you know what you are gaining by NOT seeking out your own talents, it is easier to let go of those old outdated beliefs about yourself and move on to new horizons. Think about the things that you do naturally that others say "I wish I could do that _____ (fill in the blank) as good as you do" and you say "whatever, no big deal, that's nothing, etc., etc."

Take that "(gift/skill)" which IS your hidden talent and look at yourself in the mirror and introduce yourself to yourself (a la Michelle Obama) by saying "Hi, I'm (Your Name) and I can do (whatever is your talent) which will (state the benefit it will give). By saying this aloud to yourself will literally allow you to see and feel how great you and your talent really are. I guarantee this will be a turning point for the good in your life.

A key to discovering a hidden talent is to remain open and receptive to new ideas no matter how crazy they may seem. For more than a dozen years after entering the workplace employers and clients regularly told me that I would make a great teacher. I never took the idea seriously because I could never see myself being comfortable in a conventional classroom environment. In 1985 I discovered a subject I am passionate about Reflexology and now I love teaching it because it's fun and not work.

In the search for your hidden talent try something that is completely new that you may be afraid to do. Some things like Skydive sing at a Karaoke, visit a church you know nothing about, volunteer for a crisis center, join a club or study something completely foreign to you. Break out of your imaginary comfort zone and you might be surprised what at will awaken inside of you.

How about taking a stroll down memory lane, when you were playing by yourself as a child, under the age of seven, you had such a vivid imagination open to all that you could be and do in the name of having fun and just enjoying life as you knew it to be.

This will key you into your soul's purpose. Were you a teacher, did you build things, make clothes for your dolls, or heal your pets? It is important to remember what you imagined when you were alone, and therefore un-influenced by other people, and under the age of seven when the "inner self" is more pronounced than the conscious mind and conscious ego. Here lies your hidden talent just waiting for you to bring it out into the light.

One of the ways I uncovered a hidden talent was to tune into myself. Our talents are all there but can sometimes get masked by taking jobs just to make money. Instead, we need to think about what we love doing. For example, I always a loved to write but never thought to make a career out of it. I went the practical route studying social work in college. Upon graduation, I worked in the field of social work. I knew something was up when I learned I like writing social service programs and work books rather than doing case work. After I realized that my talent and strength was writing, I started pursuing my writing career.

I have shared a few ideas to help you in your search to find your hidden talent. There has never been a better time than now to let your light shine. You are unique and have so much inside of you that the world is waiting for you to share. In your talent search focus on this, *what will be your most memorable contribution that your friends, families and colleagues will remember and say about you?* Will you leave this world taking your talents to your grave and depriving the world of receiving that special gift hidden inside of you?

Only as high as I reach can I grow, Only as far as I seek can I go ,Only as deep as I look can I see, Only as much as I dream can I be ~ Karen Ravn

---

Chapter Three Face and Release Your Fears
Dare to Dream and Go for It

You gain strength, courage and confidence by every experience in which you really stop to look fear in the face. You are able to say to yourself, 'I have lived through this horror. I can take the next thing that comes along.' You must do the thing you think you cannot do ~ Eleanor Roosevelt

Don't let your dreams fall by the wayside. Chances are to achieve your dreams and live a life you love, taking action is essential and crucial. The achievement process begins with having a deep seated desire that drives and motivates you. Napoleon Hill, in his landmark book, Think and Grow Rich, had it right. "*The starting point of all achievement is DESIRE*". Keep this constantly in mind. "Weak desires bring weak results, just as a small amount of fire makes a small amount of heat." So, your first step in achieving your dreams is you've got to really, really want to turn your dreams in a life enriching experience.

Do you have a dream deep in your heart that you want to pursue? If you do, have you taken the first step necessary to achieve it? Taking the first step is perhaps the most difficult thing to do in achieving a dream. There are a lot of mental obstacles that make it difficult to take that first step.

Here are some don'ts that helped me solve my mental obstacles:
* Don't wait until the situation is perfect. You should not wait until the situation is perfect because the situation will never be perfect. No matter how or when you see it, there will always be something that make you think again.

* Don't wait until other people agree with you. Just like you shouldn't wait for the situation to be perfect, you shouldn't wait until everybody agrees with your idea. There will always be opposition, and that is perfectly normal. If you wait until there is a consensus, you will never start.

* Don't wait until your skill is good. We might think that we need to have good skill before we start doing something. But the truth is, you will learn much more by doing than by waiting. Doing allows you to hone your skill much faster than just learning the theory.

As you can see, the three points above have "<u>don't wait</u>" in them. So here is the bottom line: the best time to start is now. I learned these skills when I started on my journey to change my lifestyle and mindset. The moment I decided to change my attitude about my life, I didn't have the skills or support I needed to begin the process nor did I understand how much I would have to give up to make the change work. But I started the life style change journey anyway. The first months were really tough. After about few months of reading every book I could find and attending online and offline seminars on lifestyle changing , I finally decided I needed to work with a mentor who could helped me move smoothly through the transition process.

Thankfully, the ups and downs of the lifestyle changing experience taught me a lot. Although each and everyday I am still learning and growing as I constantly make the necessary improvements in my life as I travel this road to achieve my dreams. It is so amazing to see what you can learn. Here are some of the things I learned how to do successfully to take my first step:

* Believe in your dream: Believing in your dream is essential to get the motivation you need to achieve it. You simply can't fool your own heart. Deep down inside you know whether or not you can believe in your dream.

* Is the dream worth pursuing? Is it something that you want to pour your heart into?

* Visualize your dream: Can you imagine – in detail – how the world will look like when your dream comes true? Visualizing your dream will energize you because you can then see how the world changes for the better and how people live a happier life because of your dream. The energy and excitement is there for you to feel.

* Expect some hard times along the way: While it's not impossible, achieving your dream is definitely not easy. Don't expect an easy way; expect some difficult experiences instead.

Having the right expectations from the beginning will make the journey much easier for you. That way, you won't be surprised and lose heart when you encounter obstacles and challenges along the way.

* Take one bite at a time: Your dream may be big (it should be!) and that might make it seem overwhelming. Like the saying "When eating an elephant take one bite at a time." So take a small portion of it that you can handle. Think about something that you can do within one week, and then think about what you can do today. It could be as simple as calling a more experienced friend to ask some questions.

In a quote by Gail Denvers, that says it all *"Keep your dreams alive. Understand to achieve anything requires faith and belief in yourself, vision, hard work, determination, and dedication. Remember all things are possible for those who believe."*

Step out on faith and give life to your dream ~ Njideka N. Olatunde

Chapter Four......... Stop the Worrying
Put the Past to Rest

We don't see things as they are, we see things as
we are ~ Anais Nin

Letting go of your past, whether that means quitting an addictive relationship or grieving a death can be one of the hardest things you'll ever do. Even if it was an unhealthy relationship, you may still struggle to move on with your life. It's not easy, but there are practical ways to let go of your past. There is a saying, *"you can not miss something that you never had"*. This must be the reason why it is not uncommon for most women to have an obsession with whatever they hold on to. Most of us have difficulty in letting go of relationships, people, jobs and life experiences we have out grown.

I am a true example of someone who has made a lot of mistakes in my life. I've often found myself thinking about the past and all the different decisions I could have made and different paths that I could have taken. I'm sure you may have felt the same way as well. Thoughts would creep up in my head like, *"If only I'd said that"*, *"I shouldn't have done that"*, *"Why did I hesitate?"* and many more thoughts like that. A perfect word to describe it would be Regret.

Regrets of the past, are just a few of the things, I discovered that was unhealthy for my mental peace. I also found that regrets wasn't the only thing destroying my mental peace. Many times I found myself so in love with someone, that'd I'd have trouble being without them. I'd feel disturbed, uncomfortable and out of place in their absence. I guess obsessed would be a good word for it. But there have also been many times, where my mental peace was disturbed not by negativity, but indirectly by my own positive actions.

I had successfully won a contract to provide wellness services to a large government agency that was to me an automatic renewal, it was my over confidence and self assured attitude that got in my way in competing for the contract at renewal time.

This was beyond confident, I was teetering between arrogance and stupidity, both of which do not represent a good place to be in. As I was going through all these life experiences it always left me feeling depressed and sad at the end of the day. It was not until I began to take some time out and begin to meditation, I realized how to go within to gain my freedom from the past. This was a way for me to achieve sustained and serene mental peace. There is no magic formula in releasing the past. It's really all about Just LETTING GO OF THE PAST. I'll say it again Just LET IT GO...

Every time something happens that agitates you, just be glad nothing worse happened and LET IT GO. Every time someone tries to put you on the spot, bless them for spending so much energy on you and just LET IT GO. Whenever you make a mistake or falter somewhere, its o.k., pick yourself up and LET IT GO. Whenever you achieve some great feat or great goal, Good for you, don't hold on to it and become egotistical. Be modest and humble and thank the universe for the blessing and then LET IT GO. Every time something happens that makes you feel fearful, anxious, uncomfortable, depressed or unhappy, focus on the good times you had in your life and LET THE BAD ONES GO.

Now I know that letting go can be difficult and to be honest, initially it is. But there were two things that really cemented the power and thought of "LETTING GO" in my mind. In understanding the concept of letting go it's all about doing what you have to do to stop beating yourself up mentally, physically, and emotionally on a daily basis. The ultimate reality is to just let it go.

To be successful in letting go begins with releasing all energy, thoughts, emotions and feelings you are holding on to. This is how I learned to clear my mind of its shackles so I could find inner Mental Peace.

I also found in letting go of a lot of negative things, I had to create a very strong positive anchor.

I focused on looking into my past (one last time for this exercise) to find a feeling so strong and positive that still had a hold on me and replace those feelings and energies with renewed happiness and bliss. To do this, is about reminding yourself of that thought and those feelings at that moment and begin to use it whenever you need to let go of something unpleasant.

I personally found that focusing on LOVE and PEACE together worked the best for me. I took the time to remind myself of the beautiful people in my life who inspire and empower me. This is what makes it possible for no negativity to measure up against the happiness I feel when I'm with my kindred connections. It's like a free spirited butterfly trying to fly into a cloud in the sky. It's just not going to happen. So remind yourself that no matter what happens, it doesn't make a difference and just LET IT GO.

Empowerment tip. To the women reading this, the time is NOW to put your past to rest. When you bury your past you can see what is real and truthful in your life. There is NO such thing as the PAST and NO such thing as the FUTURE. They just don't exist. Think about it. Do they really matter? It's not like you can do anything about it except think about it. All we can truly do is live in the NOW, this PRESENT moment.

Why waste time thinking about things that don't exist. True mental peace is when you're free from the burdens of time and are free to just focus on this moment right now. When you are able to see, feel, and know that "Now" is all we have and all we'll ever have, your life will be filled with bountiful blessing. So begin today LETTING GO OF YOUR PAST

Yesterday is dead and gone... Today is present...Tomorrow is a possibility, so all you have is Today. Learn to live each day to its fullest. ~ Njideka N. Olatunde

Chapter Four......... Stop the Worrying
Get Out of Your Head

What We Think, We Become ~ Buddha

There is a saying "You are what you THINK". Have you reached a point
in your life where you want to be rid of the continuous torture of a
"thought generating" mind? I can remember when I had that thought
and it was not an easy task to over come. Obsessive or negative thoughts
are known to make your life miserable when you are plagued by them.
But there is hope in being able to transcend your mind into being free of
suffering forever.

The mind is the root of all suffering. By its very nature the mind is
negative. 80-90% of the thoughts that the mind generates are fearful or
stressful. For some it might be 95-99%. That's when you can't stand it
anymore. Your brain is the most complex mechanism in the world, it is
certainly the most influential organ of the body, with it you think,
remember, love, hate, feel, imagine and analyze. The average brain
contains about 12 billion cells, totaling 120 trillion connections, it is no
wonder scientists say that the human brain is the most complex
arrangement of matter in the universe. Your brain has three very
important functions, your intellect, emotions and will. It is little wonder
that with all the negative input we put in our minds we have such a
negative reaction to life.

Thought control, and learning how to control negative thoughts can be
at most times very difficult, but it can be done. The tragedy many
women face is letting their thoughts consume their lives, we let ourselves
be controlled by unproductive thinking to the point of self defeat. I
have heard women say "I don't need any thought control to live the
good life", which shows denial.

Learning how to control negative thoughts is vital because it's not about
what we think we are, but it's about what we think we are not. This is a
very real question that we need to seriously look at. We sometimes
believe that we are at the mercy of what we think about or what we
allow to enter our minds, when in fact we are the "*Masters of Our Minds*".

———

This means we should use our minds to serve us and not to control everything we do. In Asian cultures such as India meditation is used for relaxing the mind, or China where tai-chi is also used as a form of mind relaxation a thought control exercise to take back control of your mind.

In learning how to take back control of my mind, I had to find and take the time to strengthen and relax my mind. In the beginning I found the thinking process was just plain hard work for me, and my results could not be measured because I was mentally lazy by nature. I always choose the path of least resistance. Once I was able to overcome this inertia of getting my mind ticking again then the hard grind was over and my thinking mind was being trained to accept me being the one who was in charge of the "Thinking Department". Our minds are a muscle that needs exercise just like any other muscle in the body, so learn to stretch your mind because what you don't use you loose.

When I was going through the thought control training program I learned that there are three stages you go through before the thought control training can become a physical reality. When we think about something we allow that thought to ponder and dwell in our minds. We react to that thought weather it be a physical or internal reaction.

When it gets to the stage where we allow it to cause a physical or internal reaction, we are too late. If we allow that thought to reach this stage which is " mental action", we end up dwelling on it until it takes a hold us mentally, physically and emotionally. We no longer have any control of our life.

Stage One: Positive Expectation
To master and archive a positive outlook on life is something we are all in titled to. Positive expectation can be either good or bad for you..... that choice remains yours.

The feeling of expectation is one that puts you in "the now" it is an expectation of good things to come, if we simply relax and know that some time in the near future you can experience a life changing event that can lead you towards your true calling in life....and purely because you expect it to.

Positive expectation also releases you from negative past thoughts, with a focus on the future and that "unknowing" something that will change your life. Remember this will require commitment and discipline to train your thinking process. It won't be so easy because negative thoughts tend to hang around like a bad smell. Practicing 10 -15 minutes a day for a week and increase your time according to how you feel. Positive expectation is a mental tool you can use for self development. It is important to use this tool whenever you can, as long as it brings you to a place of serenity and that's all that matters.

If I believe in one thing, that would be, we were not put on this earth to worry about fruitless things that will bring us nothing but grief, that affects our minds, bodies and emotions. I am a firm believer that time spent healing the mind is time well spent.

Stage Two: Thought Stopping
People may say, you don't need thought control to live the good life, well I hate to burst your bubble we "Do Need" to have control over what we think. Thought stopping has been proven to be very effective in controlling unwanted or negative thoughts that seem to clog our minds. This is by recognizing and acknowledging that we know that a thought is either going to benefit us or have a negative impact. This is crucial in the thought control process because we tend to ponder on it until it becomes so overwhelming. In thought stopping, the focus is on evaluating the thought in the beginning, like watching a movie on a big screen, you do not need to be judgmental, just sit back and watch as you look at the big screen and see all those thoughts of yours pass through the big screen.

Having this frame of mind is essential, so you don't get sucked in by what you see instead you looking and evaluating to see if your thoughts are beneficial to you or not. If it is not than you need to cut it off right there A.S.A.P. (as soon as possible).

Stage Three: You Are What You Think

Control your life, and don't let your thoughts control you, picture yourself as the person you want to be and move towards becoming that kind of person. If you see yourself a failure, than a failure you will be; if you see yourself as someone with purpose and direction then that is the kind of person you will eventually become. Never surrender your dreams to noisy negatives. You hold the key to your mind and the thoughts you think. Learn how to accept and release.

The reality of successfully achieving my goal in thought control and getting out of my head began when I took full responsibility for my thinking habits and patterns. It is a known fact that when you change your thinking your life will be so much better.

The thoughts to begin working on are the troublesome thoughts about a situation that you have absolutely no control over. Your only response is based on that crazy self-talk inside your head that serves no purpose.

Empowerment tip: Remember that Self-talk is that inner running voice that you have within yourself. It is the self talk that has you in bondage and is keeping you from achieving your dreams and living the life of a bold, successful, courageous and happy woman.

Happiness is when what you think, what you say, and what you do are in harmony~ Mahatma Gandhi

Chapter Four......... Stop The Worrying
You Make Me Sick

The beauty of life is to experience yourself ~Unknown

Living can seriously place some obstacles in our lives known as health problems. Today women of all ages are experiencing so many health problems and most women have no idea why this is happening. I will share my thoughts in hopes to lay some ground work so we can turn this around.

One of the reasons why women have so many health problems begins with spending so much time caring and nurturing everyone else that you fail to take care of yourself. When we fail to take care of ourselves, we end up in situations that result in health problems based on physical and emotional stress in our mind and body. As women, we are known to be nurturers. When we play this role we become so involved in what's going on with the people in our lives that we begin to pick up and internalize all the energy that is connected with them. We never consider that all the time and energy we give in caring for others can place a big toll on us mentally, physically and emotionally. There are studies that show stress can cause our bodies to breaking down resulting in the many health problems that women are experiencing today.

So as women when we fail to take time to recognize the warning signs presented to us and ignore them for the sake of others usually, results in the many health problems we are facing that is attacking every area of our bodies. Our health problems stem from avoiding and failing to take the time to listen to our mind and body when the messages are being sent. No illness ever happens without a warning sign. When the signs are presented to us this means you need to address the problem before it becomes a major health concern. A warning sign means you need to take some time out for yourself.

This is be very important in having optimum health and wellness. Take a moment and look at this picture of yourself always caught up in feeling that you have to do for others to the point of neglecting yourself at the expense of your health. Is this a price you really want to pay?

———

Let's begin to look what we can do to start changing this health picture. One of the ways we can change the many health problems we are facing is to first realize that we are human. The fact that we are human means we will have some health challenges and our bodies will have some weak moments as well as some strong moments. We need to remember that when the body gives us a warning the body is asking for rest and we should grant the body its request. When the body is experiencing a health crisis it goes through a healing process that is needed to bring balance and release the illness. It is important that bring your body into a state of rest and relaxation so the healing process can work. It is only through rest and relaxation that the body can heal itself.

The hidden secret to bringing the needed changes in a health problems begins with acknowledging that you need to give yourself some mental, physical and emotional downtime. This how the body begins the healing process before a health situation turns into a major dis-ease. It sounds easy but it is seen as so hard to do. To get move pass the feeling of this is so hard to do, you have to become "*SELFISH*". To be selfish means *I am taking care of my self first mentally, physically and emotionally so I can be healthy and well to care for others.*

We all know that close to 80% of health problems is a result of stress. If you are stressed you are sitting yourself up for a health problem defined as a Dis-Ease. Stress plays a big role in women's health, and the reason is because women take on whatever they are involved in with a serious commitment. It is the taking on of projects, activities, family matters and whatever else that can be seen as a heavy burden, which is internalize and becomes a stress factor in our life.

Stress is always a result of something that's going on outside of a body that we bring inside and start internalizing it. When you look at the stress in your life and connect it to a health problem it is often times associate with a situation or experience that made you sick.

The lost of a job (situation). You heard a rumor of a car accident with a family member, your mind starts reminding you of a past car accident. (experience). It is mentally moving you through a stressful experience as these examples show how stress can make you sick. When you internalize stress on the inside, it creates dis-ease. The role that stress, plays as it relates to women's health problems is when we fail to realize that everything that's going on in our life we may not be able to address or handle at that particular time. By internalizing the situation or experience it is an invitation for stress, which creates dis-ease.

The fact that we can't address or handle a situation or experience at a particular time means we have to learn how to let it go. When we fail to let it go, we always end up with our body becoming overwhelmed, and when our body becomes overwhelmed, the only way the body can protect itself against stress is to break down and creating what's defined as health problem that carries the names of a dis-ease known as illnesses that affect the body.

It is so very important for women to eliminate the stress in their lives and it can be done. When I felt the need to eliminate the stress in my life and my health problems I had to learn how to find the *valuable asset in me.* I like using the term, *fall in love with myself.* When you fall in love with yourself that means there's nobody, no thing, or no place that's more important than you. When you realize how important you are, then you begin to put the barriers up so stress cannot break through. By putting up stress barriers I have a love myself security system in place.

When stress busters come, my security system sounds an alarm to the world with a strong voice that says, I love myself and because I love myself, I'm not going to accept this experience trying to enter my life; I'm not going to accept this situation; I'm not going to eat this particular thing; I'm not going to go to this particular place because all these things contribute to the stress in my life. Because I love myself, I will not let stress enter.

In order to eliminate the stress associated with health problems, you must have a stress barrier. The barrier that you put up is falling in love with yourself. With your barrier you give honor and value to yourself by not letting anything, any person or any situation break down the barriers. Your armor of protection is "*I love myself first and foremost; I value myself first and foremost*". The one thing I recognize about eliminating stress from my life is to my body is a sacred temple. When I see my body as a temple, that means I allow only things that are precious and valuable to connect with me and I'm not letting anything come into my sacred space that's going to disturb my peace.

Empowerment tip. Remember if you want to eliminate the stress associated with your health problems "**Falling in love with Yourself**"

We often hear about emotion and illness. This is a major concern in the lives of women because we are so emotional which can be a good thing. The relationship of emotion and illness with women relates to how we act and our physical response to a situation, a person, place or thing. Whatever emotion we connect with it is the experience and how we respond to it that forces you to take action or with draw. Specifically, when it is responded to on an emotional level and can result in an illness.

Here's an example of how a situation can contribute to an illness......There is a rumor going around my job that the company is going to lay off 10 people. The fact is it's only a rumor that 10 people are going to be laid off. But all I heard was 10 people being laid off, how I respond to that from an emotional perspective is going to relate to how it can end up becoming an illness. If I respond to it from the standpoint of getting angry about being laid off and I don't know that it's really happening, all I know is 10 people are going to be laid off and I get angry just thinking about and saying I'm not going to be one of those 10 people being laid off.

So whatever I have to do and what ever it takes to stop it I will do it. It is a rumor and the self talk inside your head that has just build up all those emotions that can be a big contributor to a serious health problem by raising your blood pressure, which can result in high blood pressure or trigger hypertension if this is a present condition.

Another response to the rumor could be, I know I am one of those 10 people who are going to be laid off. All I can do is think constantly about it because I know my name is on that list of 10 people that are going to be laid off. Consistently thinking about the rumor along with internalizing the possible outcome leads to emotionally withdrawing. By focusing on the rumor with the outcome in place, now has build up your emotions and can be a big contributor to some serious health problems such as headaches, stomach aches, neck shoulder pain, low immune system and can be a big contributor to many serious health illness such as cancer, mental breakdowns, addictions to name a few.

These are a few example of how emotions from a situation happening outside of your body that you internalize can contribute to an illness. When we are only looking at the connection of the physical, mental and emotional relationship as it relates to life events and how we respond and handle them we can see the major role it plays in health and wellness. Begin taking a close look at what is going on in your life and how you can work as hard as you can to not let it stress you out. Make reducing the stress factors in your life a part of your preventive health care program.

To begin releasing the emotions connected to health problems you must not become attached to the situation, person or thing that can contribute to creating an emotional imbalance experience in your life. Yes, this may be easy said but hard to do. The truth is and I will say it again in order to release the health problems associate with an emotion, you've have to pay attention to what's going on inside your body. You can not be disconnected from you body and expect it to heal itself.

You are your body, mind and emotion. When you make this connection you are on the road to being in charge of your healing process.

When a situation happens, take a few minutes to start paying attention to how you're feeling and what you see.

Are you getting emotionally charged up?

Are you having some inner body sensation or pain?

Are you having any emotional feelings?

Are you seeing physical reactions and signs outside your body?

You've got to learn how to see and pay attention to what you're feeling.

Are you starting to get angry?

Are you getting an emotional reaction because of it?

Are you getting a physical or response?

It is so important for us as women to learn how to start paying attention to what's going on in our mind body and emotions. This is our key to having the health and wellness we deserve. Being aware and focused is called stepping outside your body to look at yourself from the outside while looking in. This is a skill that we need to learn because once we start stepping outside our bodies and begin looking with our eyes and listening with our ears we will know how to use our emotions as a healing tool.

What a rewarding experience it will be when we learn how to use our newly found healing power. We will be able to alleviate a lot of the major health problems that we're having today. When we accept who we are as women utilizing our inner healing power abilities, we will be able to make a difference in the world. Our ability to change the health problems we face begins by focusing on the number one contributor to all illnesses STRESS.

Just imagine alleviating health problems by connecting the stress factors in our lives to an emotional response based on something happening outside of our bodies that's internalized can be stopped and our bodies can heal itself like it is suppose to do. All it takes to make this a reality is for you to decide to kick the stress in your life to the curb.

Women power is a formidable force ~ Gro Harlem Brundtland

Chapter Five.........Accepting Who I Am
Standing Up For Me

Always be a first-rate version of yourself, instead of a second-rate version of somebody else ~ Judy Garland

As a woman, who chooses to stand up for herself can be very challenging if you are use to letting others have their way or are a people pleaser. Think about it, when you trim yourself down to suit everyone else, it's all so easy to whittle yourself away. When you learn to stand up for yourself it is a way of ensuring that other people respect you and don't try to push you around or manipulate you. Unlearning these old habits of devaluating self and gaining the confidence to stand up for yourself won't happen overnight but the journey for improvement starts with taking the first step. Believe me I know because pleasing people was really my first name. To stand up for yourself means that you have to learn how to use assertiveness skills. Being assertive, as it relates to standing up for yourself means you are refusing to allow someone else to have control over you. This in the beginning for me was a very frightening experience because I had for so long accepted being a victim as a normal reality in my life. Each and every day, I along with many women lived in a world of power and control influenced by oppression which creates a victim mentality.

Let's look at just what it means to be assertive, Susan Zeidman, who oversees assertiveness training for the American Management Association, based in New York City, says "assertiveness is a behavioral style of communication in which a woman can express her thoughts, feelings, wants, and needs in a clear, direct, and honest manner while respecting the rights and needs of others". For many women who avoid confrontations they are more passive in their approach to things and they often hope the problem will go away or that they won't have to say anything."

Successful women who have assertiveness skills know the importance of using this skill to build relationships, negotiate tasks with responsibilities, or work together with other people in a variety of settings.

When you understand the power of being assertive you learn how to communicate better; you have confidence; you become the decision maker; you are respected and you stay true to your beliefs and passions.

Becoming an assertive woman was not an easy task for me. In my desire to take back control of my life this was a must step I had to do. In the beginning I had no idea how to stand up for myself. What I did know, I was tired of being stepped on, looked down upon, and disrespected for no reason. Believe me when I say was a true victim, and I did nothing to stop it. My life was a living hell. I had to learn some basic techniques to stand up for myself and boost my self esteem. One of the first things I had to do was, decide what I truly want to change in my life. If you have ever been bullied or disrespected, and it has impacted you in a negative way or are tired of people making you feel miserable this is the first hurdle to overcome in becoming assertive.

This hurdle was really challenging because I had to remove myself from negative people and influences. If you have friends that belittle you in the presence of other people or just make fun of you then you need to get rid of them. To grow strong in your assertiveness skills training begins with avoiding the bullies in your life whenever possible.

When you can't avoid them just ignore them to the best of your ability. These are the people who aren't worth your time or energy. See them as people who are struggling to find themselves. Until a bully finds themselves they can not shed their stripes of being a negative and disrespectful person. When I learned how to stop, accepting and allowing bullies in my space I started to feel good about myself. This is the first lesson you must learn in assertiveness skills training. When you learn this lesson you are in the driver's seat in taking back control of your life. I found this step to a bench mark toward my progress in becoming assertive. I learned how to be confident and comfortable with who I really am and it was such a rewarding and enjoyable feeling.

By no longer pretending to be someone I was not was such a relief. There are two types of people in your life, those who will like you those and who will always give you a hard time. When you feel good about who you are, these people don't matter. Your focus is on being the best person you can be and not care at all what people think about you.

When I started doing small things every day to boost my self esteem I started to fell a sense of self empowerment. I would do things like Volunteering my reflexology services at senior citizen centers, or just simply let a driver get in front of me if they needed to, which are all small things that in the long run helped make me feel better and stay on the path of standing up for myself. In applying this step it was a real eye opener for me. I had to learn how to speak up when people disrespected me and I had to be willing to leave my imaginary comfort zone to let others around me know they were being disrespectful and it is not acceptable. I had my first experience to practice this skill with a person in the grocery store who cut in front of me while I was standing in line. They shouted to the cashier "Excuse me but I need to buy these things now" ring me up.

When I said I am next in line and you can not cut in front of me, you need to go to the back of the line". She was speechless, because her actions were based on figuring out she could do it and get away with it. My speaking up proved her wrong. I was scared but I said what was on my mind and it felt really good.

In taking this action, I found it to be very empowering because I was able to up the ante on my people pleasing traits by not just sticking up for myself but sticking up for others around me who were being treated unfairly. This was a small power play victory for me. Being able to see a person back down because I spoke up for myself was an enlightening experience. What made the experience more real for me was being able to speak up for the group of people who were all in agreement but unable or had not learned how to be assertive by standing up for themselves and not being taken advantage of or humiliated. It is so important for women to learn how to stand up for themselves.

If it is your desire to live the dreams in your heart it begins with being assertive. When I learned and applied these very important skills it made a big difference in my life and my ability to pursue my dreams. Take a moment to think about these life changing skill and how it can work in your life.

Believe in yourself. If you don't have confidence in yourself, it will be difficult to succeed in anything; people don't look up to or respect a person who is incapable of exuding self-confidence. It's easy to spot a person down on their luck and lacking in self-confidence, and mastering self-belief is the first step to standing up for yourself.

Change your attitude. Your attitude is everything and will impact how other people perceive you, right through to the signals you're unconsciously sending out. Your attitude sets the tone of your voice, the quality of your thoughts, and is reflected in your facial expressions and body language. Remember attitude is infectious. If you're bubbly, happy, and bright about things, you'll encourage those around you to feel good about themselves and the world around them. If you're morose, pessimistic, and down about everything, you'll soon infect others with the same negativity. We naturally prefer to be hanging around the person who makes us feel good about ourselves, and we're more inclined to listen and respond positively to someone who has a good attitude; by the same token, we're more likely to dismiss a person who tries to play the shrinking violet, the victim, or the permanently oppressed. Make the choice to put on a positive attitude around others and you're on your way to standing up for yourself.

Seek to undo the damage wrought by life's hardships. For many women an inability to stand up for oneself is rooted in a series of experiences in life which resulted in negative outcomes that were turned inward, and became a reason to put themselves down around others. The reality is that everyone experiences life's vicissitudes; it's how we respond to them that changes everything. By choosing to take the negative occurrences personally and to retreat into your shell, you stop standing up for yourself and start letting life buffet you about.

Taking action can be as easy as making a decision to stop taking negative things personally, but for most people it requires working through the resulting negative thinking patterns and learning to reroute them.

Some key things I had to learn and keep in mind included:
* Beware of staying in the victim mode

* Beware of taking passive aggressive responses toward people and situations because a passive aggressive approach to life will never enable you to stand up for yourself.

* Beware of resorting to aggression

Trust your instincts about other people and act on them. If someone doesn't feel right for you, don't hang around them; be courteous but don't be a doormat. You don't owe difficult people any explanation for your need to spend less time around them. Avoid bullies, negative Karen's, and sarcastic Nancy's. You don't gain anything by being in their presence and they're not doing anyone favors by taking out their own inadequacies on other people. Keeping away from sources of discomfort and trouble is not running away; it is still very much about standing up for yourself because it demonstrates that you won't let nonsense and nastiness impact your life.

Turn the negatives into positives. Another way of standing up for yourself is to take the negatives thrown at you and to transform them into good things. In the process of turning attacks inside out to find the good, you're often unearthing jealousy or insecurity from the person who threw the put-downs your way.

* If someone claims you're bossy, rather than letting it cause you to shrink some more, take this as evidence that you're a natural leader, able to manage people and projects well, and a proactive change agent.

* If someone claims you're shy, take it as a compliment that means you're not ready to jump on the latest bandwagon but like to reflect over the consequences first and then make up your mind.

* If someone says you're too sensitive or emotional, let this be a sign that you've got a big heart and aren't afraid to let everyone see it.

---

* Or maybe someone suggested you're not career-minded enough – for you that confirms you're living a stress-free life that will help you to live longer

Don't give up. No matter how hard you try to improve yourself, to come out of your shell, and to increase your confidence, there will be days when you feel that you're backsliding. Feeling sick, a bit blue, or tired, are often reasons for feeling that everything is on top of you. Rather than seeing this as a defeat in your attempt to learn to stand up for yourself, see it for what it is a day or so where things went off the tracks temporarily before you feel better and bounce back.

Some tricks I learned to use to get through the learning curve included:
* Fake it till you make it. Even if you don't feel confident, act as if you do.

* Be consistent in your approach. People will grow to expect that the person you are now is a person who stands up for himself.

* Expect some people to find your more assertive stance challenging. It can take time to reshape the patterns you've formerly established with people who used to walk all over you. In some cases, you'll find you no longer want to be a part of their lives; take it as it comes. Be consistent and always focused.

Think about the information and apply them whenever possible. You will gain the respect of others and be a happier woman living her dreams. This is a call out for all women on a mission to become the woman they are created to be....accept the challenge and start today by *"Standing Up for Yourself"*

Champions have the courage to keep turning the pages because they know a better chapter lies ahead ~ Paula White

Chapter Five..........Accepting Who I Am
Defining Who I Am and Feeling Good About It

Each day that I wake up I get to choose how to
live ~ Esther Brady Crawford

In the morning when you awake each and every day you should always feel good about who you really are you are, because you are a Phenomenal Woman. What does it take to feel good about yourself first thing in the morning? When you look at yourself in the mirror what and who do you see? To feel good about yourself begins, with taking care of your beautiful body. Yes I said beautiful body because the body you have is beautiful inside and out. Do not let anyone tell you anything different. When you take care of your body, you feel good about who you are as a woman. You may be saying you have not seen my body. I say to you, why have you refused to take care of the body you think is not beautiful?

In asking this question I have found there are many reasons why women refuse to take care of their bodies. One major reason has to do with if "I'm always labeled as being fat or too skinny, why should I be obsessed about taking care of something that does not look so good". If all I see is a picture perfect body as defined in accordance to how Madison Avenue says I'm supposed to look, then that is a big joke. The reality is mentally and physically I'm not there so the end result is I do not have a beautiful body. If this is what you see and feel, it means you just don't care about your body because to you it will never be picture perfect. When a woman feels helpless about her body she usually resolves to do nothing to change or improve herself. She feels that all she can do is compare her body to the standards of what society says she should look like.

By choosing to accept this as the gospel she sits herself up for failure. The down side to refusing to take care of your body is a big price to pay, that leads to the many health issues that affect your body's well being. When you refuse to take care of your body, you are refusing to accept who you really are. When you refuse to accept who you really are, then automatically you have no respect for your body.

If you do not feel good about your body, you can not respect how you see yourself or how others see you. There are so many women today who refuse to take care of their bodies, they have lost the ability to see the spirit inside that shines the light of hope, love and joy. To lose the spirit that dwells within, leaves you with a feeling that says "I just don't care about myself anymore". This is a picture of a woman who doesn't feel good or care about who she is. She just wants the world to know this is who I am accept it. If we turn this around into a positive it will be you accepting and defining who you are. How your body looks has nothing to do with being able to feel good about who you are as a beautiful woman.

If the image of who you're supposed to be is based on what Madison Avenue says, you have the right to accept or reject it. You have choices. With those choices are responsibilities. You can look at yourself and love every inch of who you are. Define and set standards for your self that you can live with comfortably. You can also look at yourself and hate everything about how you look. You can let society beat you down because you don't fit the Madison Ave mold. The choice you decide is the one that will define or devalue who you are as a woman.

Empowerment tip: If you are ready to start taking care of your body one of the first things you can do is, when you get up in the morning and look into the mirror and tell yourself that you are beautiful.

You will need to say *"I am a Beautiful Woman"* each and every day in the morning. When you say these words, this begins the process in taking care of your body. It is the power of these words sending a message to the brain that is transmitted to every organ, cell, tissue, muscle and bones in the body that you're taking care of your body. By acknowledging through the power of your voice with words that affirm you accept and respect who you really are, a beautiful woman. If you want to make some changes to your body, you still need to respect and accept who you are to achieve the desired changes.

It is all about accepting self that opens the door to confidence and being able to do the things needed to improve yourself. You can start by doing small things to improve your health, because as you improve your health you will also be improving and taking care of your body. Look at it this way, you can see yourself moving towards achieving the desired body you have defined for yourself. The picture you see when you look at your body shows that you feel good about yourself, and when you feel good about yourself you are taking care of your body, mind and emotions. When you take the time to take care of yourself you will begin to have the beautiful body you desire.

In taking care of my body I also needed to take care of my mind, because my mind and my body work hand-in-hand. When I say to myself mentally I'm beautiful, when I say to myself that I'm feeling good about my body today, I've given my body the fuel it needs to feel good because my mind has shared that message to my body and through that message, I now can put a smile on my face and when I smile and say I am a Beautiful woman, I love myself and I accept myself for who I am today, I have now taken care of my mind, my body and my emotions to do the job of working with me to become the Beautiful Woman I Am Created to Be.

I have shared with you what I use to help me stay focus on how I see and define myself each and every day. For me it doesn't matter what Madison Avenue says I'm supposed to look like, this is how I look and I feel good about who I am, how I am, where I am and what I am today because I've taken care of my mind, my body and my emotions. Every day I remind myself that I look good, I feel good, I am beautiful and I do not need anybody else to say or tell me who or what I am. It is up to me to be in charge of defining who I am, taking care of my body and accepting who I am by living life to its fullest letting the little girl in me come out and play.

We are not what we know but what we are willing
to learn ~ Mary Catherine

Chapter Five..........Accepting Who I Am
Become the New Chief In Charge

*I think the key is for women not to set
any limits* ~ Martina Navratilova

My personal belief and the belief that you'll find throughout this book is to empower woman to take back control of their lives and begin to live lives filled with happiness. We all have experiences and stories about getting close to or giving up on living the life we really want. When we look back at what happen we can find a lot reason that stopped us. The truth is nothing and no one stopped us from achieving our dreams. There is only one answer to this question, "What has stopped you from living the life you really wanted to live"? The answer is *You and only You.* The number one reason you have not achieved your dreams is because you decided to stop pursuing it. You were not willing to take action in spite of your fears. You accepted fear; you got comfort with less; you lack the ability to be confident, powerful and strong and you rejected taking a risk to successfully achieve. I can say these things because this was me before I decided to change my mindset and lifestyle.

It is a major life changing decision when you decide to taking back control of your life. What you are doing is deciding that you are the only one who will be in the driver's seat, not anyone else. In choosing to become the new Chief In Charge requires some serious sacrifices that most women are not will to do. Cutting back on people, places and things, changing living arrangements and style, living on less, and reassessing your life purpose and passion is what is needed to live the life you really want. The reality is you have to move away from your imaginary comfort zone to achieve the successful results you want.

This message I am sharing with you, is the same message that was given to me to make the necessary life style changes. This is the action plan to do if you want to become the New Chief In Charge of your life.

It can be done and it doesn't matter if the economy is good or bad, your relationship is sliding down hill, your health is not the best it can be, your children and family are giving you the blues, or you are feeling in the pits, this is called life and the lessons it is to teach you.

The good thing is no matter how negative things seem there is always a positive side. Here are some of the rules I used in turning things around in my life so I could start the process in taking back control of my life. My ultimate objective through out the whole process was to become a powerful, confident and successful woman doing what I want to do and not what everyone else wanted me to do. Before I share my rules, I want you to know when I began the training program I wanted to quit many times because my imaginary comfort zone was being challenged and I was basically afraid of achieving what I wanted. This is the point in my life where I connected with my passion and purpose. When this happens there is no turning back.

Rules to guide you in redefining the life and woman you want to be:

* Challenge yourself to use every 'bad' thing in your life as a new beginning.

* Find the 'good' in everything that you can.

* Don't expect the good things to be readily apparent. It may take a few days, weeks or even months before you finally see them.

* Allow yourself to realize your true power. This doesn't mean pushing people around, but looking for your hidden skills.

* Talking to yourself is a very powerful tool to use and it can help you increase your motivation and your ability to stick to a task.

* Stop expecting others to solve your problems. Even if you lost your job it's an opportunity to look in a new direction, to acquire a new skill and to blaze a more pleasurable path in life.

* Throw away that "yes, but" expression from your life. It's just a way of keeping yourself stuck in the mud.

* Take a good hard look at what you'd really like to do and have in your life. Sit down and begin making a list that outlines the steps you need to take. Not everyone needs to go to college to be happy. Find out where your happiness lies, if you don't want to go back to school. Abraham Lincoln did just fine with his self-learning plan.

* Beware of the negative people in your life. Pointing out the problems is fine, but some people only see doom and gloom and they can't be very helpful, unless you find that helpful.

* Remember that every road has unexpected turns and that any plan must be one that allows for some give and take. If there's one word for your plan in taking back control of your life, let it be 'flexible' and go from there.

For the woman who is ready to say "YES" to being the new Chief-In-Charge. I welcome you to this exciting journey.

With every step that you take, know that the road will sometimes be challenging but with each step the end result will be the peace, harmony and strength needed to turn your life around. You become the new Chief-In-Charge, an empowering woman who aims to inspire women with the courage to break free from the chains of limiting belief patterns and societal or religious conditioning that have traditionally kept women suppressed and unable to see their true beauty and power. There is no better time than now to *"Go For It.... Take Back Control of Your Life"*

I am Who I Am...Be Good To You ~ Author Unknown

Be Yourself ~ Truthfully

Accept Yourself ~ Gracefully

Value Yourself ~ Joyfully

Forgive Yourself ~ Completely

Treat Yourself ~ Generously

Balance Yourself ~ Harmoniously

Bless Yourself ~ Abundantly

Trust Yourself ~ Confidently

Love Yourself ~ Wholeheartedly

Empower Yourself ~ Prayerfully

Give Of Yourself ~ Enthusiastically

Express Yourself ~ Radiantly

Chapter Six.......... It's a Family Affair
Parenting Aint Easy

It is really asking too much of a woman to expect her to bring up her husband and her children too ~ Lillian Bell

Being a parent is not easy especially in the age of single parenting. To be a woman who is a single parent it is challenging and frustrating because you are being a parent by yourself. So when you're parenting by yourself you don't have a back up system and you often feel so overwhelmed.. You are faced with emotions and feelings of not being able to really do all the things that are required in terms of being a good parent. The reality for most women, who are single parents, is dealing with the number one basic issues if you have preschool children, enrollment in an affordable early childhood program or daycare center that will meet your time schedule requirements.

If you're dealing with a child who is in school, just being able to handle the things related to your child and school responsibilities can be a difficult task. One of the single parenting responsibilities that women constantly face is the idea of being responsible for someone other than themselves and someone whose livelihood actually depends on you. This is the number one fear for single parent moms. A big reality factor that can be devastating emotionally, physically and financially is caring for a child with health needs. When you think about caring and meeting the health needs of a child is a big stress factor for a single parent mom.

I know first hand about this, as a single parent mom, with my son who had an illness they could not find a diagnosis. They preformed many test with one test being a spinal tap. As a single parent mom I could only think of two things my son's health and the expense of the hospitalization. This is a difficult state of affairs for a single parent mom because the only thing that is important is for your child to be healthy and well no matter what the price. I had to make a decision to take charge and become the healing force needed to restore wellness to my son. When I made the choice my son's health was restored. To this day they never were able to give me a diagnosis for the illness and he has never been sick like that again.

Despite all the challenges and frustration of being a single parent mom there are some very rewarding experiences. The most rewarding experience for a single parent mom is the mere fact that your child is an extension of you. The fact that your child is an extension of you, means they are a special person in your life that you will work with in helping them to grow and develop to their fullest potential, and that's a rewarding blessing. When a child that you are caring for can come to you and say something that can lift your spirits or make your day, a rewarding and cherishing moment, make the challenges of be being a single parent mom null and void. When a child can come to you and show you something that they have created and they think about you in their creation, that's a memorable and loving experience that gives true meaning to you being a mom.

The reality to look at in being a single parent mom, despite all the challenges, are the things that you can hold onto as you nurture and help your child grow and develop from infancy into an adolescent, teen, and young adult. This is the real experience that makes parenting worth all your time, energy, tears, and love. The fact that each and every day when you wake up and you see that smile on your child's face, or every day that you can just touch that child in a special way and that child can touch you back, that's your reward for being a single parent mom.

As children grow into finding their own identity, single parent moms are faced with problems of communicating with their children. I learned about this problem with much frustration. One of the things I discovered was I did not know how to listen. I found that the number one reason communication is such a problem with children is because we fail to listen to our children. Most of the time, we see children as being little people, but they are people that have ideas and feelings. They also are people that are struggling to communicate to their parents about the things that are bothering them. I discovered that because I did not listen to hear what was going on inside my son's mind, I was a big contributor to our communication problems.

My failure to listen resulted in my son giving me the silent treatment because he knew it would annoy me to the max. I had to learn when my son said something to me and I didn't understand what he was saying, not to speak for him or turn what he was saying into something that was not the fact, if I wanted to improve our ability to communicate with each other. I found out that if you're telling a child to do something and that child does not understand what you're saying or asking them to do, you have a communication problem.

If all of a sudden your child becomes defiant, what's happening is a communication problem, because the child's does not understand what you're asking of them or they do not fully understand exactly what you want them to do. So a lot of times parents communication problems are a big result in failing to listen. We need to learn how to take the time to listen to our children and allow them to share their thoughts and feelings freely with you. You may not agree but it is a good thing to know how to listen openly so you can learn what's on your child's mind. When we learn how to listen to our children, we also teach our children how to listen to us and that will alleviate a lot of the problems related to communication and help establish a real parent child bonding experience.

Now you know the real importance of parent child communication the next step is how to effectively communicate with your children. The most common way for mothers to effectively communicate with their children is to create what's called "*Say What's On Your Mind Time*". I created this for me and my son and it worked wonders in improving our communications and relationship. During this time period I just let my son talk. I let him talk about anything that he wanted to talk about, all I did was listen. This is how I learned how to be a good listener. This is a skill that has to be learned because most people do not know how to listen all they know how to do is just hear words.

When you are able to really listen to your child you have earned their respect and taught them how to be confident with an ability to speak and share their feelings.

The power and energy between you and your child during this time is an experience you will always hold on to because listening to your child allows you to learn what they're thinking, what they're feeling and what they really want.

This is an excellent activity to do with your child weekly. Pick a day and keep that day and time as a special time exclusively for you and your child. It is important not to let anything interfere with your *"Say What's On Your Mind Time"*. Remember to see this time as a parent child bonding moment. This special learning time teaches your child how to openly communicate their feelings, wants and desires.

Throughout the ages their always has been mother daughter relationship issues. To improve this relationship begins with respecting each other as females and respecting each other in terms of differences. When you talk about mothers and daughters, you're talking about two unique females coming together revealing exactly who you are. It is also about, as a mother, not to look for your daughter to be a carbon copy of you and for your daughter to not look at her mother as being someone who's outdated and doesn't know what's going on in today's time.

For mothers and daughters to come together and have a positive and rewarding relationship that can be a win/win for the both of you, means respecting each other with open and honest feelings. A good place to being is to look at each other's differences and find something good about it that can foster growth and development. In finding something good in your relationship means to look at the good times and how the two of you are able to see something beautiful and positive in the experience that is a reflection of mother and daughter and daughter and mother. I think when we look at how we are different and defining the beauty in that difference is what allows us to express ourselves fully as mother and daughter, and daughter and mother. In other words, when we mirror each other we can see each others differences and see the good in it.

When mothers and daughters are able to acknowledge their differences they are on the road to improving their relationships. To begin the process mothers and daughters must learn how to have and spend some fun time together. I don't think a lot of mothers give thought to doing fun things with their daughter or see it as something that is needed and really important to do. When a mother and daughter can have what's known as fun days, which can become play days and the play days can be turned into days of reflection and cherished time together, you open the door to creating a powerful mother daughter bonding experience.

For a mother and daughter to improve their relationship, each must have and pick their day for openly sharing feelings in a non judgment way. The mother will have a day to say this is what I want to do with my daughter today and pick an activity that can be mutually agreeable for the two of you. The purpose of the activity is to learn how to enjoying each others company and spend some fun time together. It could be just a girls' day out, where the two of you go to the spa and have a whole day that' allows you to bring out the feminine mystic inside of the both of you.

The daughter does the same thing, coming to the mother saying this is what I'd like to do today, would you share in this activity with me. This can begin the process in improving the relationship because it's about sharing in an experience that you like and want to do together as mother and daughter. The ultimate objective is to open the lines of communication to start sharing likes and what's important with each other. It is through such an experience that an improved mother and daughter relationship is something you can look forward to. In looking at the struggles or any stress going on in a mother and daughter relationship by creating a special time together will make a big difference. I think instead of saying improving the relationship we should consider how to strengthening the relationship. When a mother and daughter can have their relationship grow stronger in terms of reconnecting and re-bonding one with each other this is what is most important.

Empowerment tip: Mother-Daughter bonding time is good for mothers with adolescent to adult daughters. The idea to start the process is what lays the foundation in opening the lines of communication that can be a memorable moment for the both of you. It can also become a mother-daughter family legacy that can be passed on for generations.

As a mother with a son who has experienced some of the things that mothers do that can cause their sons to be rebellious and difficult. I know this to be a fact and it is a big no-no to share negative feelings about your son's father with your son. If you want to avoid the negative emotional roller coaster to hell with you son heed this advice. In my work I have seen this destroy many women who are single parents raising their sons. Usually when the son and even daughters begin to become rebellious it's always about some type of stress as it relates to the mother and her relationship with the father that spills over to the children. It can be a negative remark, action or comment that gets the ball rolling in the eyes and mind of your son. The biggest thing that can cause the most rebellious situation between a mother and her son is how she presents the image of the father to her son. The reality in your son's mind of his father is one of importance, respect and being a valuable asset in his life. Until a father proves himself differently a mother can not change the thoughts that her son or daughter has for their father.

When a mother displays, negative emotions or thoughts about a child's father, theirs a heavy price to pay. I have seen many mothers shed tears, lose everything, experience emotional and mental break downs because of children involved in rebellious behavior and actions. The two most challenging experiences for a single parent mom with a rebellious child are incarceration and death. For a mother to find peace in her relationship with her rebellious child, she has to always, no matter what the differences are that exist between her and the father, she must always be neutral with her presentation to her son or daughter when talking to them about their father. The reason is because to your son and daughter, regardless of what exist between you and him, they see themselves as an extension of their father.

It is a fact, that, whatever or however that son or daughter feels about their father, its their feelings and it should be respected by the mother. If you disrespect the father with your son or daughter, it usually will result in the negative and rebellious feelings that in the end will wind up hurting the mother in the long run.

As a single parent raising your son or daughter by yourself, regardless of how you feel about the father you will need to eat crow, when you talk about their father to them. You conversation should be about positive things and experiences. When you take this approach your son or daughter can develop a relationship with their father, which is important to them. Through time they will decide for themselves how they want to relate to their father. This will be a star in your crown because you did not cut them off from having a relationship nor did you constantly share your negative opinions.

Empowerment tip. Remember to alleviate some of the rebellion, you need to be open, honest and truthful in your conversations with your children about their father. Never say anything that is attacking or downright negative in your conversations with your son or daughter as it relates to their father. Trust me, this advice will bring peace to your home and create a healthy and stable relationship for you and your son or daughter.

The father son relationship specifically for single mothers dealing with rebellious sons is centered on anger toward the mother. To a male child he sees his mother as the reason the father is not in his life. Mothers, do not take this as a personal attack. A child does not know all the reasons and facts that created the situation that the father is no longer in your life. So the child has to blame someone, what better person than his mother the person he sees and is close to everyday. The question is what can mothers do to help their sons release the anger that's behind the rebellious behavior?

In raising my son as a single parent mom this was a hard pill to swallow. For most mothers it is a double edge sword. You having to deal with the father and all his mess and the negative feelings your son has toward you, it's a big downer. In a situation like this the top priority is helping your son to get over his resentment and anger.

The one thing I did to help my son release his anger, was to allow him to express his feelings and not to take whatever he said to me as a personal attack.

In going through this process I found out how much my son loved his father and how deep down inside how hurt he was that his father was no longer in my life and we were not a real family. I had no idea that my son had been thinking a lot about his father, family and my relationship with his father. Just like what I shared about mother and daughter having some special time together, mother and son need to do the same thing and create some reconnecting time together. This will help your son to feel comfortable in sharing his feelings and no matter what he is feeling, he can come to you openly and honestly to say what is on his mind.

When your son can openly share his feelings with his mother, then he is able to freely release all the pent up anger, hurt and pain. If you son does not release the anger, the end result can cause some serious life changing problems such as legal issues resulting in incarceration or death, mental and emotion health issues or just overall physical health concerns because of bottled up anger. Mothers to aid your son in finding peace in his life you will need to allow your son some venting time. All you need to do is sit and quietly listen.

Just let him release those pent up feelings so he can let go and find peace. When he has completed his releasing, sit with him and calmly talk, with your child, about what you and he can do together about what he feels and help him to understand that by sharing his feeling is how he can begin to heal and start feeling good about himself and life.

The one saving grace for me in my relationship with my son was that I always talked to him giving him a sense of empowerment so it was not like me being the one in control. I made it a point to remember how important it was to let him feel that he still had his power and dignity as it related to his feelings and my reactions. What was most important was the end result, helping him to deal with his feelings of anger and learning how to let go and move forward with his life.

Remember always that you not only have the right to be an individual, you have an obligation to be one ~ Eleanor Roosevelt

The parent-child relationship is one of the longest-lasting social ties that human beings have established," said Kira Birditt, a leading social family scientist. In her studies she said "This tie is often highly positive and supportive but it also commonly includes feelings of irritation, tension and ambivalence." Knowing how to cope with difficult parents as an adult child will help you find happiness and peace in your life. Here are a few tips I have shared with my clients in dealing with toxic parents that have help many of them overcome childhood difficulties and achieve their life goals.

How to Cope With Difficult Parents – For Adult Children
* Build Good relationships. Adult children of difficult parents need to know how to build good relationships with them period, even if your mother or father doesn't accept who you are. Remember: even the most unorthodox childhood can be a springboard to success – depending on your attitude and perspective!

* Become Aware of Your Feelings. "When we're not aware of what we're feeling, the feeling becomes the master," writes Sue Patton Thoele in her book, *The Courage to be Yourself.* "A repressed or suppressed emotion builds up power until it's impossible to contain and, as a result, erupts destructively."

In the long run, however, swallowing your feelings about your childhood or difficult parents can lead to anxiety, depression, physical illnesses, and unhealthy relationships. Violent eruptions become more likely, such as emotional meltdowns over computer glitches and screaming fits over lost keys.

If you're coping with difficult parents as an adult child, you need to find healthy ways to express your feelings. Think let go and release.

Take resentment, for instance. Maybe you feel rejected because your mother or father smothers you or keeps "lending" thousands of dollars to your brother. Maybe your mom nags you to lose weight, get married, clean your house, or get your hair out of your eyes (your thoughts are oh, to have a normal mother!). Avoiding your feelings of anger or resentment because it does not pay off so why do it? Avoiding negative feelings is easier, less painful, and requires less energy — in the short run.

* Accept Your Feelings. Knowing and accepting your feelings brings freedom and a stronger connection with difficult parents. As an adult child, simply saying out loud, "It aggravates me when mom tells me how to discipline my kids or dad always telling me how I should spend my money" can be a very liberating experience.

Resisting your feelings makes them stronger; accepting your feelings makes them manageable. I advise my clients to talk openly about their difficult parents. In one of my session a client shared that when she was in high school her mother regularly visited her at lunch time. She described her mother as having her own make do hair extension and wore dirty, baggy street-person clothes. By seeing her mother, come to her school, resulted in a daily battle of humiliation and embarrassment, for years, as a child and throughout her adult life. Every day for years those feelings, grew and grew just like compound interest. When she couldn't take the pain anymore she turned to self-destructive ways as a form of release.

For her the end result was simply a feeling of despair. The reality of the experience although it was bad in the end her feelings lost its strength and it became easier to connect with her difficult mom because she realize and accepted her as who she is her parent.

* Practice Forgiveness. Oprah recently said that "forgiveness is releasing the hope that things could have been different". True forgiveness is realizing the gift in a bad childhood and learning from it. Every experience you've had makes you who you are and makes you more yourself.

Your unique personality and spirit wouldn't be yours if you had different parents or siblings – even if you got a bad deal. Coping with difficult parents is easier when you accept and let go of the past. Sometimes that means letting go of someone you love.

Forgiveness is easier when you accept that your parents did the best they could

*You don't choose your family. They are God's gift to you,
as you are to Them* ~ Desmond Tutu

Adult sibling rivalry often starts with childhood sibling rivalries, which are two very different types of family conflict. Fighting with grown brothers and sisters is quite different than childhood conflict.

When you're a child, sibling rivalry or childhood conflict teaches you how to relate to others, sometimes for good and sometimes for bad. Either way, your adult relationships are definitely affected by your grown brothers and sisters. If you're struggling with adult sibling rivalry, your experiences can change how you communicate with your partner or children.

Mom always did like you best!" Sound familiar? If you feel strained in your relationship with your family because your parents favor another sibling, or another sibling's family, you may be surprised to find that you're not alone. While most parents love their adult children, it's surprisingly common for a parent to be closer to or more supportive of, particular adult offspring over others, sparking sibling rivalry. In my practice I have found it to be also common for a many of my clients to feel that a particular sibling is or 'has always been' favored by their parent, even if this may not be recognized or acknowledged by the rest of the family.

For some of my clients, getting along with their siblings seems impossible. With a canyon between them filled with wrongs perpetrated on each other through the years, they feel like they will never find common ground.

It is those old childhood wounds, genetics, parental attentions and life changes that can have alter the relationship between siblings. The true test of blood is thick than water reveals that there is hope. Here are some tips I advise my clients to use in rebuilding a positive sibling relationship.

95

Stop making the tally marks. That is, stop comparing their possessions, their successes and failures with your own. Instead, learn to celebrate their joys and support them through the heartaches.

* Choose not to compete. You don't need to constantly prove your value as an adult. Just let it go and relax. Nobody needs the stress of constant competition.

* Get over being angry and realize that you aren't feeling anger, you're feeling hurt. Communicate with your sibling how their actions are hurting you without yelling or getting upset. Stay calm and clear in your communication.

* Build up your own self-confidence. This will help with ending your desire to compete with your siblings and will also improve as you end comparisons. Know that you can handle whatever kind of reaction or response your sibling has to your open communication.

* Share your needs with your siblings. Allow yourself to be vulnerable. You can't create the relationship you want if you don't communicate what you want in the first place.

* Know that you'll be okay if they don't reciprocate your interest. At least you'll know you put forward the effort to make things right. You've given your siblings the option when they're ready.

The real truth behind sibling rivalry is an unspoken bond that will always exist. Who else has known you your entire life and can bare witness to your strengths and weaknesses despite the dysfunctional family experiences? Sibling relationships run deep, even though, at times, they may seem like they barely skim the surface of our lives. We all deal and see our childhood experiences in different ways. In our relationships with our brothers and sisters we come from the same lump of clay that is our childhood and has shaped us into becoming a unique human being, which is a miracle in itself.

Despite our individual struggles, triumphs, joys and disappointments, as sisters and brothers we are made of the same stuff that defines who we are as family, whether figuratively or literally, from the beginning. It is through our challenging sibling rivalry that we can come together to explore our truths and gain a compassionate understanding that no matter what as a brother and sister we are one.

Sibling relationships - and 80 percent of Americans have at least one - outlast marriages, survive the death of parents, resurface after quarrels that would sink any friendship. They flourish in a thousand incarnations of closeness and distance, warmth, loyalty and distrust ~ Erica E. Goode

Chapter Seven.......... Relationship or Situation
Letting Go Is So Hard to Do

When women are depressed, they eat or go shopping. Men invade another country. It's a whole different way of thinking ~ Elayne Boosler

When it comes to ending a relationship it is filled with so many emotions that it feels like a hurricane has hit you. For women being in a relationship is something that is very special and sacred. Being in a relationship is how a woman defines and reveals her true essences. When a woman enters into a relationship she opens up like a flower sharing her inner and outer beauty. She gives of herself freely mentally, emotionally, spiritually and physically. When a relationship comes to an end, she has suffered a great lost her most valuable asset the gift of sharing her love. So the question is asked how can women learn to let go of a relationship that has come to an end.

Having gone through the experience of a few relationships coming to an end it was really hard to let go and say good bye. In looking back at the experiences I see them now as a life lesson in Relationship 101. To learn what it takes to be in a relationship you have to be taught by the master teacher who is the creator of relationships. Your teacher always sends someone into your life for you to learn the relationship lesson. This lesson can be a harmonious one or it can be a turbulent one, the outcome is always yours to choose.

When a relationship has come to an end for whatever reason, you need to be able to realize that if it's come to an end, that means it's time to let it go. There is always an inner knowing when something is wrong in your relationship. The only way to learn how to let go of a relationship is when you feel that the person you have been in a relationship with is now worthy of your friendship.

You are saying yea right, you don't know my story and my pain. The truth is we all have similar stories and the relationship ending concept is the same. It is time to let go and move on.

In accessing your relationship as you move from being lovers, you can still be friends. The reason you can be friends is because whatever brought the two of you together, you started as friends, so why can't you end that relationship as friends?

If we take the time to look at the lesson our master teacher has given us we will learn that although the relationship has come to an end with that person who was our mate, lover, and significant other we have grown and evolve into becoming a new woman with beauty and substance. When you can step outside of yourself and see who you really are as a person you have learned your relationship lesson. The lesson learned is to end the relationship means, you and your significant other can be friends and if it is time to let go and move on you can do it. Together you have given a new meaning to your relationship that allows you to have inner peace.

The reality of the relationship is to remember all the time that you spend together was for your good. During the time you spent together you were both able to grow together, you were able to become who you are in terms of where you are now as a woman and a person. All of these experiences are what contributes to your growth and development into how you have become who you are right now at this particular point and time in your life.

Empowerment tip. As women going through the difficult time of ending a relationship, it is so important that you understand in letting the relationship go on a positive rather than a negative gives you back the freedom to be your true self. When you can wish your significant other the best, will allow you the opportunity to move on to another phase of your growth and development in the lessons of life.

Chapter Seven.......... Relationship or Situation
Emotional Roller Coaster

Well-behaved women seldom make history ~ Laurel Thatcher Ulrich

As I think about my past relationships I see myself riding on an emotional roller coaster with lots of ups and downs coming fast and suddenly. When faced with these relationship situations it throws you in tail spin and you don't know what to do or say at that exact moment. This is a time in your life when you are feeling your lowest and most powerless as a woman and human being. This is the most important and very crucial life lesson in a relationship that you must learn. If you fail this lesson you continuously repeat the lesson over and over again until you pass. The reality is many women live a life time repeating this lesson never knowing that the master teacher cries every time they fail.

The first lesson begins with a mate that you selected to come into your life. I say you selected, because every woman has what I call a *"Mr. Cutie Story"*. This is that dream heart throb person that you connected with for all the wrong reason you defined as "being in love". Come on ladies you know you had this person in your life. This is called *Relationship Initial 101*. In the end the outside appearance did not match with the inside. For many, myself include this turned out to be an abusive relationship. An abusive relationship is not always physical it can also be mental and emotional. The question is always asked why do women accept and stay in an abusive relationship.

I have found in my work and even with myself one of the major reasons women we stay in abusive relationship is because we have low self esteem. When you are told all of your life that you are not that, you're not worthy of this, you don't do this, you don't do that and what good are you how does that make you feel? If you keep hearing those statements over and over again you accept it as the gospel. When you want to be in a relationship with someone who will that person be?

When you want to be in a relationship with someone who will that person be? In the beginning the relationship starts out everything is great and then all of a sudden, when everybody gets comfortable inside the relationship, that person begins to push your self esteem button taking you back to that old tape already planted inside your head saying you're no good, you're not this, you're not that.

Suddenly when this happens, you go into a shell and when you go into that shell, you open yourself up to all the abusiveness be it mental, physical, or emotional. Myself, like a lot of women have fallen into this trap because it's a trap that we put ourselves in as a safety cushion. When we are in this safety cushion it's our protection and imaginary comfort zone that allows us to accept the abuse we've been told over and over again through out our lives. So once the tape starts playing, we hear the code words reminding us that" this is who I am and I can't do any better than that because this is who I am".

In my journey to break free and stop the abusive relationship experience in my life, the first thing I had to do was to find the courage to redefine myself. Finding courage is not easy to do when you have low self esteem. Your life and who you are is defined by someone else. It takes a lot of courage to just step outside of what you feel is comfortable. The steps I had to take in finding the courage, was to find someone that I could feel comfortable with in sharing my thoughts and feelings. What I was most in need of was to find someone who would not say anything to me. I just wanted someone to listen to me as I shared my feelings.

When a woman is at this point and she wants to be open and honest about her feelings the one thing that she does not need is someone responding or giving her advice. She just needs to talk so you can release all the pain, hurt, anger, and emotions associated with having low self esteem and being in an abusive relationship.

The next thing I did I was to find time to write everything I felt and experience in all my abusive relationships. It is important to write about it because it reveals a pattern that is always the same and never changes. I spent a lot of time just writing.

Whatever the feeling was I would just write and I didn't try to qualify or examine it. This was the cleansing process I used in releasing my low self esteem label.

This is the process that I used and share with my clients *"Talk about it.... to talk it out.... and write about it.... to write it out..."*. At the completion of these steps you need to allow yourself to deep breath and release it. There is healing and cleansing power in breathing. I know many of you are saying all this sounds good but I don't know if this will work for me. Yes it may sound good but the reality is, it is not easy because it's a choice that requires discipline and practice. Building self esteem to overcome an abusive relationship is not anything that you're going to do in a hour, day or month that is going to change the abuse in life instantly. For some it may take a few years. You will have to work on releasing low self esteem as a daily life time habit.

Empowerment tip: In the past every time you were facing an abusive experience, your normal response would be to accept it. When you are ready to accept a new reality get quiet and take that moment to verbally release with someone or writing it out. Always remember the choice is yours to accept or reject the abuses that hold your self esteem as a hostage.

I found that by getting into a habit of doing this process it became my foundation for building my self esteem. When you build your self esteem you are in charge of what feelings you will accept. For women in an abusive relationship, the dynamics are the other person has a false sense of power that is used to control you and your feelings. In building your self esteem you take away the ability of another person to control how you feel. The moment you're able to verbally release your feelings with someone or write your feelings down on paper you take away their power over you.

If you saw the movie *What's Love Got to Do with It* starring Tina Turner, she had low self esteem. She eventually found a process to build her self esteem and take back control of her feelings. This is what you will need to do to end the abusive relationship experiences in your life. When you can verbally release your feelings or physically write you're feelings down you have taken a giant step in building the self esteem needed to remove yourself from abusive relationships mentally and physically.

You have to accept whatever comes and the only important thing is that you meet it with courage and with the best that you have to give ~ Eleanor Roosevelt

When we understand how we get into an abusive relationship the next step is to look at why we keep attracting negative relationship partners into our lives? In the work I do with women and looking back on some past relationships the one thought that comes to mind is, if you feel negative about yourself, then you cannot do anything else but attract that which you are feeling. Remember I said you will continuously repeat Relationship Initial 101 over and over again until you pass.

For many women who keep attracting negative partners into their lives is because they keep failing the relationship lesson. They fail the lesson because they feel negative about themselves. To change the relationship attraction dynamics you need to know that you cannot bring anything or anyone new into your life that you don't already have inside you. In the relationship lesson we fail to understand that the person who becomes our relationship partner is a mirror reflection of who we are. This is a real problem for women because who you want and attract into your life is usually a reflection of your negative self. If a woman does not feel good about herself, then she cannot attract a man who will feel good about her or toward her.

I learned this lesson after repeating this class a few times. A change can not happen until you learn how to stop feeling and being negative in every area of your life personally and professionally. When you are always saying negative things, if you're always seeing negative things, then that's all that is going to be in your life and that's the relationship partner you will constantly keep attracting in your life. Remember the saying *"You Are What You Think"* it is true. Look at what you're thinking, feeling and saying in addition, to the image you are projecting of yourself.

What you see is the energy you are sending out into the Universe. It is the Universe that responds to your request for a relationship partner. If your energy is always negative then negative is always going to come back to you.

To change what we want in a relationship partner means you will have to really focus on this fact, *am I being negative* and *if I am, I must understand that until I change my negative behavior, I will keep attractive negative partners into my life*. When I decide that I don't want a negative partner in my life then I have to look at how I can turn being a negative person into becoming a positive person.

To turn being negative into being positive I had to believe it, see it, and feel that I was a worthy person. I had to seek out the good in me. In doing this I am giving power to the positive in me. Think about this, if you are always seeing the downside, then you can not build yourself up.

Empowerment tip. Who is the best person that can validation you, NOBODY but YOU? So it should not matter how anybody else sees you or what they feel about you, because you're the only one that can validate how *good you are*. So each and every morning you awake and when you look in the mirror, you need to acknowledge that you are beautiful, you are self confident, you are self worthy and you are the best person in the world today. And only you can say that because that's who you are.

Nothing in life is to be feared, it is only to be understood. Now is the time to understand more, so that we may fear less ~ Marie Curie

Usually in most relationships there are memories some good and some not so good. In working with women I talk about the need to forgive and forget. The response is always "*why should I forgive or forget my significant other with all the pain and hurt he has done to me*"? One of the things I have found is that for many women when a relationship has gone bad there is a lot of negative and painful emotions stored up and held so closely to the heart. It is the pain and hurt that is constantly on the minds of most women and makes it so hard for them to forget and forgive their significant other for the hurt they feel.

I refer to this experience as the *Emotional Roller Coaster Tape* which is played over and over again reminding you of all of the negative things that were said and all of the negative experiences you have gone through. As you relive the relationship through the daily mental reminders, it becomes so very hard to even give a thought to forgiving or forgetting. By holding onto to the hurt and pain nothing changes and it becomes detrimental to you mentally, physically and emotionally than it would be to forgive and forget.

I'm not saying to dismiss it as if it did not happen. What you need to do is take a serious look at what did it happen in your relationship and why it happened. By looking objectively at your relationship you can discover some amazing things about yourself. This is not an easy thing to do. It is easier to stay stuck in the feeling sorry for yourself victim mentally. I know because I did it. You have heard the saying *"misery loves company"*. You can always find another woman who will join you in the victimhood pity party.

Going through being the victim experience, was not a good thing for me because it was destroying me and my health. I had a reality shock that turned me around quick fast and in a hurry, I'm in ill health and my significant other is healthy and moving on with his life. This was the wake up call I needed. It became time to do some inner soul searching which lead me to understand the importance of forgiving and forgetting.

I found that when I could look at why the relationship was no longer working, how and when it did happen, I began to understand that we had out grown each other and it was okay. In gaining an understanding of my role in the relationship changing, I asked myself the question what am I supposed to learn from this experience that will make me a better woman, that will make me a stronger woman, that will even help me to be a more confident woman? This was my life relationship lesson that I had to learn so I could pass my test. The test question I had to answer on my life relationship lesson final was, being in this relationship with my significant other, no matter how bad or difficult it may have been, what did I learn about myself?

One of the things important in helping women to learn how to forgive and forget is to reflect on when you first got together because there had to be something happy and positive that brought you together. It is a fact that we get so caught up in the negative that we forget to remember the happy times that brought you together and moved you to the point that the two of you no longer spend any happy times together. There are many factors that may have contributed to this change in the relationship. A big change that is often so difficult to understand, the two of you have out grow each other and for whatever reason it's time to let go. This is an eye opening experience that many women do not want to face or accept.

When you are facing this relationship hurdle with resistance you create a situation that becomes negative and painful. The reason is because your relationship role has changed and there is no longer a need to be in this relationship as each other's significant other. Another factor to consider is, it may mean that the dynamics of each other's needs in the relationship has changed, which can be very hard for most women to accept. This is the real painful one that leads us to holding on to the hurt, pain, and frustration.

Here is the truth kicker about this type of relationship experience, a lot of times as women, we know when the relationship has come to an end or is at a turning point that a change needs to happen. This is where we play the victim and we hold on and don't want to let go by denying the reality for whatever reason.

When you are on the relationship emotional roller coaster you need to get back to the point where you are able to look at your relationship noncritical for the sole purpose of letting go the hurt and pain so you can move on with your life.

Empowerment tip. Being in a relationship is probably one of the most challenging life lessons we as women must learn. The only way we can master the lesson, pass the test and not keep repeating this lesson for numerous times is to always keep in mind. what brought the two of you together and what got you to the point that you are no longer on that same page with each other as mate, lover, and significant other will help you in learning how to forgive and forget.

When one door of happiness closes, another opens; but often we look so long at the closed door that we do not see the one which has been opened for us ~ Helen Keller

One of the biggest obstacles that most women face in their relationships with their significant other is a breakdown in communication. A major break down in communication between women and their significant other is the fact that most women do not know how to listen. It is important to hear with understanding what is being said to you. Failing to do this means lack of communication. When we're talking to someone, usually we're not listening to them. We're hearing what they're saying while preparing as they are speaking to give a response to what was said to us. So if we're preparing to get a response, we only heard a certain phase or a certain part of the conversation. And that certain part of the conversation is usually something that relates to a trigger point that automatically is saying I need to respond to this right now, meaning I didn't hear the essence of what you're saying to me. I only heard some negative and disturbing words.

This is a big communications problem in all areas of our lives. We never hear the message of the sentences that are being shared. By not hearing the message you have a breakdown in communication. When there is a communication breakdown, what is being said through partial hearing has triggered into something that usually will wind up becoming an argument or a disagreement. The reason is because you didn't take the time to listen to the whole conversation, let that person finish what they're saying, so you can respond to all that was said and not just a specific part of what was said that you interpreted.

The major culprit in a breakdown of communications is power struggle. It's about who wants to be in control of what was said or something that was said hit a nerve that you did not like and automatically you have to respond to defend yourself. As women, this is a major life relationship lesson that we fail to learn, everything that's said to you does not necessarily mean that it has to be responded to or you have to verbally defend yourself. This lesson is failed and repeated on a daily basis. Until we learn how to listen non defensively with an open mind so we're able to communicate constructively, we will always have a breakdown in communication.

Communication is an art and a skill that when learned can be an asset in helping women improve what and how they speak to their mates in their relationships. One of the things women can do to improve their communication skills in their relationships is to practice the art of not talking and just listen.

This is a hard one because women have the need to talk and explain themselves. It took me quite awhile to master this skill. When you have low self esteem you are always in a defensive mode. Being defensive means talking and explaining yourself. This will require lots and lots of practice. As you practice this skill it is important to remember that you do not have to be on the defensive about everything all the time. Learn how to say yes to *"I may be wrong, but if I'm wrong this is what I'm willing to work on changing that."* You can score a big A+ on your life relationship lesson assignment with this empowering communication skill.

In developing your communication skills stop seeing yourself as always being attacked. When you learn how to communicate with a listening ear the person who is seen as the attacker is diffused. This communication skill is so valuable in building your self esteem. The master teacher will be so pleased that you have learned the art of listening lesson.

With this communication skill you will be able help your significant other see you as a woman to be respected. Communication shared about your thoughts or wanting something from someone begins with you needing to offer encouragement instead of discouragement. When you share praises that uplifts instead of always sharing something that pulls a person down will always opens the communication door to give you what you want.

The major problem connected with a breakdown in communication in a relationship, usually is associate with wanting a person to change. If you're trying to get your significant other to change you have to come to them with a "peace offering".

A peace offering is presenting what you want in a non threatening downgrading tone or presence. "It takes sugar to get honey...If you use venom you will get venom". If you want change, then to get what you want means you have to change the way you are communicating your message. How you speak and what you are saying is all in your tone and presentation style. This known fact is the number one cause in the breakdown of communication in relationships with women and their significant other, *"to get what you want learn how to communicate a sweet message instead of a bitter one".*

The steps you can take to begin the process to improve your communication skills is to practice.... practice... practice

* Practice looking in the mirror and share with yourself something really happy that you want to share with someone else

* Practice smiling when you're communicating with someone.

* Feel good about yourself when you're talking to someone.

Theses are the things that can help improve your communication skills and build your self esteem. Feel good about You. Smile. Uplift yourself and others. Have the feeling of confidence when in a conversation with someone. You want to be a woman who knows how to communicate effectively with desire and passion.

To do this means you need to be assertive. Do not be afraid to be assertive it is a good thing because it will get you the results you want and deserve. It's your time to be assertive with a positive flair to it. Bring back the eloquent female side of yourself that is nurturing and caring, but with confidence. And with confidence you will have the improved communication skills you need when talking to your relationship partner

Empowerment tip. When you speak to them with confidence that radiant's a ray of sunshine flowing through you, no matter how bold it may sound to your significant other, they will respect you because the bottom line is you want to be respected in terms of your feelings and what you have to say. It is only through respect, that you and your relationship partner will be able to talk to each other when there is a breakdown in your communication.

Kind words can be short and easy to speak, but their echoes are truly endless ~Mother Teresa

In the monthly empowerment support group for women I facilitate in my practice, a topic was presented for discussion on "Do women really know what they want as it relates to being in a relationship"? As I listened to the response from the group I discovered that most women do not really know what they want as it relates to being in a relationship. It was revealed that many women's idea of what they want in a relationship is based on what the media presents to them, what they may read in a love story or see in the movies, an imagined concept of their parent's relationship or what they see in the relationships of close friends.

What was revealed in the group discussion was that women have no idea or self knowledge of what they want in a relationship with their significant other. Many women enter a relationship that is defined by their partner or society. The unspoken reality was revealed as the women in the group found out for themselves that most women do not know what they want in a relationship. The question was thought provoking and hard to truthfully answer. I concluded from the discussion that the only reason women don't know what they want in a relationship is because they have never asked themselves this question.

By women not even thinking about what they want before they get into a relationships shows they do not see who they are as a person or woman. It is a known fact that not until you know who you are, you can't know what you want from somebody else when you are in a relationship. So most women do not know what they want from the person they are in a relationship with. The reason is because they have not defined who they are or what they want from the relationship.

I can speak with first hand knowledge of being involved in relationships that I did not ask myself or even consider what I wanted in the relationship. Just being a relationship was all that was important. When this is your relationship reality you will have lots of life relationship lessons to learn. Your master teacher will give you some heavy relationship experiences as your test to pass or fail. The only way you can pass this test is to define for yourself exactly who you are and know what it is you want before begin a relationship. This is what opens the door to having a healthy and loving relationship.

113

I had to learn how to define who I am base on all of the qualities that made me feel good about myself. You have to seriously ask yourself these questions:

* What is good and positive about you?

* What makes you feel good about yourself?

* What quality or characteristic do want your mate, lover, and significant other to have?

In answering these questions the lesson I learned was that defining and identifying your qualities, you're able to define the qualities of what you're looking for in a relationship so the two of you can be a complement to each other.

Let me share what I mean, if you are a person that feels happy, you wake up every morning happy and you acknowledge that you really feel great today or you acknowledge the day is going to be a great day. You want to find someone who has the same kind of qualities. They feel good about themselves when they awake in the morning. They do everything to prepare for a great day throughout the day and share that experience with you.

This is why before you start a relationship it is very important that you and only you define all of your best qualities. You need to define all of the things that make you feel good. When you can define your qualities, then you will know what you want in your relationship. These are also the qualities you want to see in the person you want to be in a relationship with. How you define yourself and your qualities are how to find that significant other person with comparable qualities that complements you and defines what you want in a relationship.

The bottom line is whoever you're entering into a relationship with, see them as being a complement of you and you a complement to them. Know this, they are not a carbon copy of you. You both complement each other. This is known as the *mirror reflection*.

Empowerment tip. *As I see you, I see the me in you.* The main thing to want from a relationship is to accept and respect each other as you are. This is another life relationship lesson that is not always going to be an easy one to learn. The road will not be smooth and the challenges you'll face will be difficult and very trying. It is important to keep in mind, that two of you are not carbon copies of each other. You are two unique individuals with differences

.

You can pass this life lesson when you know what you want in your relationship. Knowing what you want is when you can see the reflection of yourself in your relationship with your significant other. To accomplish this task begins when you can define the beauty you see in each other and say with conviction what you want in your relationship.

Empowerment tip. In answering the question do women really know what they want as it relates to being in a relationship, can be answered when, a woman starts honoring who she is by saying what she wants in her relationship. For women who are or not in a relationship and want an A+ on the life relationship lesson final exam, learn to use the mirror reflection approach, *"As I see you, I see the me in you"*. This is the lesson you must learn if you want to be in a relationship filled with lots of love, peace and happiness.

Joy is what happens to us when we allow ourselves to recognize how
good things really are ~ Marianne Williamson

Chapter Eight.......... Taking My Life Back
It's Time to Change

She who believes is strong; she who doubts is weak. Strong convictions precede great actions ~ Louisa May Alcott

Changing our lives for the better begins with a choice. This means letting go of the things that no longer serve us taking small, but significant, steps in the direction of the life we want to live. Change has a considerable psychological impact on the human mind. To the fearful it is threatening because it means that things may get worse. *To the hopeful it is encouraging because things may get better. To the confident it is inspiring because the challenge exists to make things better"* King Whitney Jr. We all have big changes in our lives that are more or less a second chance. Being a woman in today's world we surely need a new lease on life that can be our second chance.

For many of us we see change as being uncomfortable and difficult, it inevitably involves pain, and that to change your life is to struggle and fight against the status quo. Yet we are willing to move through our lives shackled with old out dated life experiences we readily accept because we think we can't do anything to change it. Just the thought of the word change can create a emotional uprising. In the real world everyday change happens. Look at nature, world affairs, our neighborhoods, our bodies, our relationships it is all about change. Yet we fear, resist, avoid, and hate change.

Let's take a close look at what is change. Change is the process of becoming or doing something different. In order for something to change you must have a reason and that reason is TIME. In the bible it speaks of a there is Time for everything.

Time has always been about CHANGE. To change your lifestyle is a process that takes time. We must learn this life lesson 101 experience by letting the change process take its ever loving time to manifest itself. It is a step by step process that will require patience. If you have little or no patience you will not see the new lifestyle changes take place and this means you will fail your assignment.

Your master teacher will re-send the lesson to you again and again until the patience lesson is learned.

Change is all about you and the life you are living. For many women who see their life in a negatively way, this is the first change that is needed. Some of the things my clients have found to be helpful in changing the negative way they see life is to know that they are students in the class of life. As a student each day you will be given a new and unique life experience to learn. The lesson will always be challenging, trying and difficult. Your understandings of the instructions are based on how you define your life experience assignment. Will be a negative or a positive one. Your master teacher will grade you on how you handle your assignment. So the best thing that a woman can do to change the negative way that she see's life is to awake each and every day seeing life filled with lots of promising possibilities, opportunities and experiences as a new lesson she must learn.

I am not saying that every day you will like or accept the lesson you need to learn. You are human. You will either challenge your teacher or you will not do the assignment. When you do this you will always repeat this class, until you pass it. Sometimes this lesson can take a life time to learn or you can go to your grave never learning this lesson. It is so important to remember each and every time a life lesson assignment is given to you, no matter how it comes, there's always something in that experience you must learn.

Whatever it is you must learn, you need to see it as not being something that is negative. It's something in the experience, that you do not understanding and not until you understand it, can you pass and be given a new life lesson to learn. This is the school of life, where you learn through real life experiences. This is a real on the job training. Yes, the process may beat you down but, we also know, that today it beats you down but you get back up tomorrow and deal with it again. You're going to keep dealing with it.... and dealing with it.... with the fortitude of I want to learn it so I can move on.

Empowerment tip. Focus on learning this life lesson assignment so you can move on to a new life lesson. Once you are able to see the experience from this perspective, it is no longer seen as being a negative view of what's happening to you. When, you stop the negative way you see life by understanding and accepting that all of your life lessons be they good, bad, positive or negative are happening to you for a reason. The reason is to help you grow mentally, physically, emotionally and spiritually into becoming the woman you are created to be.

A life of reaction is a life of slavery, intellectually and spiritually. One must fight for a life of Action, not Reaction ~ Rita Mae Brown

Chapter Eight.......... Taking My Life Back
Making Lifestyle Changes

Life's challenges are not supposed to paralyze you, they're supposed to help you discover who you are ~ Bernice Johnson Reagon

Whether you are in or just starting the process in making a lifestyle change, it begins with one small step in the right direction or a big leap of faith. It is important that you have a sense of purpose and mission for the desired lifestyle change you want to pursue. Keep your eye on the prize as you move forward. There may be many setbacks along the way to side track or tempt you to stop know that this is a natural part of the transformation. Just keep in mind that it is temporary.

When we take a good look at what it takes to make a lifestyle change, we often see the task as being so overwhelming. This means breaking habits that are normal activities that bring us a sense of comfort. We mentally see making a lifestyle change as being very hard to do because we live in such a fast-paced society. Things come so quickly that we're caught up in the reality and drama of the things that are happening to us each and every day. Once we get caught up in the things that are happening to us, we want instant gratification and immediate results. We fail to realize that whatever situation we are in or whatever problem we are facing, it has a starting point. Nothing that happens or is happening to us each day just suddenly happened overnight. It has to have a beginning.

For most of us we go through our daily lives moving on and on failing to pay attention to the starting point of a situation or experience that is happening to us. This is a life lesson assignment that we fail to look at and study. So our master teacher adds to that assignment another little situation that you may look at and say okay, and do nothing about it. This is when your master teacher sees that you need a reality check. You now face a life experience that has blown up into a big crisis situation that you are looking at and saying how did I get into this or why is this happening to me?

By not focusing on the situation during the infancy stage, you get caught up in a full-blown crisis web. The truth is a change was needed and you were given the tools to make the change and you refused to do it. When we fail to focus on the infancy stage of a situation we create the drama in our lives that seems to require immediate results, immediate gratification and immediate answers that we can't come up with it, which makes making a lifestyle change so hard.

To learn from the school of hard knocks, which I have, caused me to see life and making lifestyle changes, so hard and challenging. I was constantly saying "*I can't get out of this situation, it keeps happening over and over again to me*". All I could see was the drama in my life and my only solution was the band-aid effect cover it up. To me this meant I would not have to look at it, take any responsibility for it or do anything to change the situation. The life lesson I failed to learn, by not doing my assignment during the infancy stage of all the drama, was to not change a stressful life experience that required commitment and some hard work.

Some of you may be saying how can releasing my resistance to change stop all the drama in my life. This doesn't make any sense to me. I say to you right now it may not make sense because this is a new way of seeing how to make a change in your life. If you want to overcome or change a troubling life experience, it begins when you understand and recognize who you are as a woman.

What you need to understand is who you are, how you arrived at where you are in life, how you are a survivor in this stage of your life and now a change is needed. When you can do an inner self assessment you will begin to recognize the need for change that leads to growth and development in making a lifestyle change. When we understand that the change that is ready and waiting to happen is nothing but another life experience we must go through so we can become strong and empowered women in full control of the life you want to live.

If it's a change that's going to help you become bolder, more confident, have more self esteem, and become more beautiful, you need to understand that your resistance is blocking your growth and development is becoming the woman you really want to be. When you resist change you are also blocking your ability to achieve what it is you are created to achieve. Your resistance also blocks your ability to do all the things you really want to do and keeps you from have all things that are in store for you to have. It is not until you learn how to release your resistance to making needed changes in your life, that you can have what you need and want to begin living a fun filled life.

I have found with myself and the many women I work with, that the biggest road block in making a life change is living in the past. For many women, holding onto the roadblock of the past to avoid change is because living in the past is something that we can see, feel, and even in some cases we can hear.

Here is what makes this real for us, If I can see, feel and hear the past, the roadblock is not allowing me make a lifestyle changes. If I never cross over into today, I will never ever get to tomorrow. To stay in the past is always a constant reminder of a mental tape in your head of what has and can happen again. The replaying of the mental tape is what makes and keeps you stuck in yesterday's blues so you can never live fully today in preparation for tomorrow.

A big problem about living in yesterday is it is a thing you cannot change. What you can't change means there's no movement. If there's no movement, you are not living up to your fullest potential which gives meaning to your life. To always live each day in yesterday allows you to be a death watch security guard. Yesterday is dead and gone. To spend a life time living in yesterday's past and never, ever living in today is a high price to pay to live a life repeating a lifestyle change lesson over and over again. This is the one lesson that really upsets your master teacher when you fail to do the assignments and learn the lesson.

So, until you are willing to move the roadblock to yesterday and cross over into today, you will repeat this lesson until you learn it or go to your grave never learning this lesson. I know you may not like that statement but it is a fact many women live their lives full of angry memories about the pain, hurt and disappointment of yesterday. For many women they die taking the experiences of yesterday with them never ever living one moment in today. Take a minute and think about how many women you know who are living miserable lives because all they talk and think about is something that happen yesterday? I work with these women and I had to work on myself to make this needed change.

So the question is how can women learn to release the past so they can move forward? Some of the ways you can release the past so you can move forward begins with awaking each day with one new and uplifting thought that's not connected with anything that happened yesterday. You can do this mental exercise to begin the process in cutting the yesterday mental cord tape from playing "Life's Past Experiences", by letting an inspiring first thought set the tone for your entire day.

Empowerment tip. To begin your day with a yesterday experience must now be seen in your minds eye as old and no longer useful news. When you start your day with your first thought in the morning being a new idea, a new thought or new experience, allows your mind to focus on creating new possibilities for lifestyle changes. When you get to the roadblock turn away and step into the new experience. When you take this action you have learned a lesson in how to release and let go of the past so you can now live fully in today.

It is a great feeling of relief when you learn this life lesson. To release and let go of the anger, hurt, pain and disappointment is true freedom. When you can bury the past and not yourself you have stepped over the roadblock with a new found appreciation for living in the now and present moment.

Empowerment tip. In learning this lesson you awaken every morning in *"thankfulness"*. This can really earn you an A+ from your master teacher, when you awaken and your first words are *"thank you for this new day"*. This means you acknowledge today and not yesterday. It's now a new day with no room for yesterday's memories.

For me in learning this lesson, each and every time during the day when I experienced a situation, or was just moving through the day and a thought from yesterday crept in, the first thing I always say is *"This is a new day with no room in my mind for yesterday's memories"*.

The fact that we are human and need to master this lesson, our master teacher likes to send pop quizzes from time to time as a refresher course, you will constantly need to keep telling yourself it's a *"New Day Today"*. This is what will eventually kick yesterday's memories to the curb so it will no longer be a part of your today. When yesterday is not a part of your today, you have begun the process in releasing the past so you can now move forward into living the life of your dreams.

In beginning this process, know that the number one thing that holds many women in bondage from making lifestyle changes begins in your mind. When I say your mind, it's the thoughts you think that your mind turns them into your reality. You are what you think, and it is those thoughts that become you and your mindset. You and only you can define who you are. When you define yourself with a negative self image this is who you become. If you visually see the mental images of you being weak, unworthy, lack confidence, having low self esteem, having doubts and fears you are mentally, physically and emotionally being held in bondage that will not let you make any lifestyle changes.

This life lesson assignment is about how you define who you are as a woman and person. The definition you use to define yourself is the key that can lock or unlock the cell that holds you in bondage. To pass this assignment your master teacher will grade you on what you think of yourself and how you see yourself. This is a very valuable lesson you must learn. Your thoughts are all you have and they can build or destroy you. Your thoughts about yourself is what how you present to others.

The image that you present to others is what will be reflected back to you. If your defined thoughts project a negative image this is what will be reflected back to you and will keep you locked in bondage, under the illusion that you have no way out. Think about all the drama in your life, which is the result of what and how you think about yourself.

Until you understand the importance of *"you are what you think is real and is a powerful life giving force"* you will always be riding on the emotional roller coaster of life. If you like all the drama and riding the emotional roller coast, hold on to your negative self thoughts. If you are ready to say yes to defining who you really are, *"Change Your Thinking"*. Learning to change your thinking will give you another A+ on this assignment and make your master teacher smile with joy because the thoughts you have about you is who really are.

Empowerment tip. Letting go of yesterday's blues and changing your thinking is what it will take to release the shackles that are holding many of us in bondage and keeping us from making lifestyle changes. To release the shackles holding us back from making lifestyle changes begins with a two-letter word that most women are afraid to use and that word is **"NO"**. When women learn how to say no with meaning, feeling and passion, they will have been given the key that unlocks the shackles holding them in bondage. Here is an example you can understand, look at the one first words a child learns to say with understanding and love saying it...... the word NO.

Think about the children in your life and there's something you want them to do and they don't want to do it, they immediately say no and think nothing about it when they say no to you. A child can say no very freely without thought or reason. As women, we need to learn how to have that same child experience, as it relates to things that affects our mind, body and emotions. Letting the little girl inside assist us in making lifestyle changes can be an enjoyable experience. In learning to say no, we need to understand that this is the key that unlocks the shackle and gives us freedom.

To achieve the desired results you need to say "NO" with passion like children do. It is power in the word no that allows change to happen that leads to living a better quality of life.

Making a life style change begins with becoming the woman you're supposed to be. When you become a woman who is able, ready and willing to make your personal contribution to the world it will require making some lifestyle changes. It will not be an easy, fast, or uneventful experience. Your master teacher wants you to learn all the required lesson steps because you have a gift and talent that the world is waiting and ready for you to share. This is your only reason and purpose for all the life lessons you are experiencing. Each day you are given an opportunity to release the shackles that hold you back from making lifestyle changes that can make a difference in the world.

It is the responsibility of every woman, who is a graduate of the school of life to come together and help other women who are in the same shackles and bondage that you once were in. These women need and want to hear from you. It is through the lessons and experiences you learn that gives you back your inner feminine power.

Empowerment tip. Whatever you are passionate about this is your life mission to share with a world that is waiting and ready to hear from you. You were given your very own personal life lesson key that unlocked your shackles and released you from bondage. You understand the importance of letting that little girl passion out and saying the word NO to anyone or anything that tries to break your spirit. You accept, think and feel good about *you and who you are.* You have learned to live life to its fullest making needed lifestyle changes so you can have a better quality of life. You are now ready to pass the baton to another woman, so she too can learn her life lessons and fulfill her dreams and passions just like you did.

I've come to believe that each of us has a personal calling that's as unique as a fingerprint - and that the best way to succeed is to discover what you love and then find a way to offer it to others in the form of service, working hard, and also allowing the energy of the universe to lead you. ~ Oprah Winfrey

Chapter Eight.......... Taking My Life Back
I'm In Love with Me

If you aren't good at loving yourself, you will have a difficult time loving anyone, since you'll resent the time and energy you give another person that you aren't even giving to yourself ~ Barbara De Angelis

The ability to love yourself is a hard thing for women to do .We spend a life time loving every one else, while hating ourselves. We have lots of issues about ourselves that no one really cares about except us. A big issue for woman is our appearance and body that hinder us from thinking positively about ourselves and hold us in bondage. This is nothing but negative self-talk that should be replaced with seeing what is beautiful and wonderful about the woman we are.

To love yourself doesn't happen by luck or the grace of the Universe. You have to create it. It begins with having a glowing vision of living life to its fullest. When you have a vision, of the life you want to have and live, it helps you tackle the core beliefs about yourself such as the doubts about your own worthiness for success that have held you back. This is the time in your life that you need to peel back the curtains around your core self belief system and tap into the life lesson skills and training leaned about change so you can successfully falling in love with yourself.

A big challenge many women face in learning how to falling in love with self is finding things we like or love about ourselves. The thought of feeling good about ourselves is often seen as being selfish and for many women this is a big "no-no". Women of the baby boomer generation culture, we're taught that praising ourselves is selfish and wrong.

This has been a big stumbling block for women who have low esteem. I found this lesson to be the hardest for me to learn. I did not feel or see anything good in me as a person or woman. I lived a life controlled and defined by society and others. I had to learn how to praise myself for things that were good about me. I did this by asking others to help me identify my good qualities.

This was a real healing experience for me to do, that was very nourishing to my self-worth. This mindset change shows that when you love yourself, you're happier and more connected to your inner self...and your new found happiness and ability to be free spreads to others.

To learn the love yourself lesson, your first assignment to do every day is think about something that you like about yourself, or something that you did today that made you or someone else feel good, no matter how small it may seem. Schedule time daily to give yourself the same kind of warm praise that you so freely given to others. Your master teacher wants you to know that you are worthy of receiving the highest passing grade for this lesson, which is done when you learn to love yourself.

In order to know about love, we've read about it seen it in a movie or someone showed us a glimpse of it. Right? Wrong. We are born knowing unconditional love. It is a gift, a birthright given to us from the very beginning. It's the conditioning of our souls taking on a human form that limits our belief to unconditional love. As we move from childhood into adulthood unconditional love has been erased and replaced by conditioned thoughts of the world. We learn that our actions cause reactions. We learn that we are either good or bad. We learn what is acceptable and what is not. This is becomes our point of reference is removing us so far away from the universal gift of love we were born with.

Through time and the many life lesson experiences, we have loss that loving feeling and it seems hopeless in attempting to get it back. It is true that seeing glimpses of it in movies and books confirms in our hearts that unconditional love does exist. We are told that it is only a fantasy. This is just a fantasy we are craving. Not true. Our spirit is craving what we have always known from our humble beginnings, "*Love Thyself*".

You need to take some time and learn about "unconditional love because it is the essence of your life. When you discover for yourself the true essence of unconditional love you will no longer depend on the validation of love from someone else.

It is only when you aren't clear on what, how and when will your needs and desires be met, that your expectation will depend on someone else giving it to you. When you follow this path you will always be disappointed. You are always placing other people in a position to let you down while they have no idea what you are expecting from them. When we are unable to express our needs in a clear manner no one understands what you want. If it is not clear to you it certainly will not be clear to them.

Finding your true unconditional love means finding the true you. When was the last time you really focused on finding out who you really are? In the school of life you are taught an in-depth lesson on unconditional self-acceptance and self-love. So what is unconditional self-acceptance and self-love? Before you can truly love yourself you must learn with a skill of mastery unconditional acceptance and love for who you are as a woman.

When you learn to accept and love yourself unconditionally it is to:

* Place no condition on yourself as to how to behave, what to do, or who to be in order to receive self-acceptance and self-love.

* How you feel when you accept and love yourself unconditionally; Negative consequences of the lack of unconditional self-acceptance and self-love Replacement out dated belief systems.

* Placing no conditions on other people as to how they behave, what they do or they are in order to receive acceptance and love from you.

When we love ourselves unconditionally we don't dwell on past events. We don't make the past the focus of how we see ourselves. We see the past as life lessons that help us grow and develop into become a whole woman and person. To love is to forgive. This is a core lesson assignment we must learn. When we can be kind and forgiving to ourselves we are better able to do the same with others. Unconditional and forgiving self-love fosters unconditional and forgiving love to others.

How you feel about yourself has a lot to do with how others feel about you. Sometimes how people feel about themselves shows in their appearance. If we feel negative mentally, physically and emotionally this is what others see in us. When we turn these feelings around to show positive feelings, the world reflects these feeling back to us.

Loving yourself is your foundation for living. In order to have a loving relationship with others we must have a loving relationship with ourselves. In working with my clients I shared with them the questions I used that helped me change my mindset:

* What would you do if you believed you were completely responsible for the presence of love in your life?

* What relationships would you heal?

* How would you act if you believed you were the source of love in any encounter?

* How would you change the way you treated yourself?

Taking the time to ask yourself questions about you, reveals your inner most feelings. When you get to this phase in your life lesson training you are ready to receive some advance training assignments. These assignments can really challenge you mentally, physically and emotionally. This is where lifestyle and mindset changes on unconditional love for self are taught.

Think about this, if you keep giving to others without giving to yourself, it is like pouring water from a glass. If you pour and pour without ever refilling it, eventually, it will run dry. So, if we are like that glass, how do we refill, recharge, re-energize, and replenish ourselves, so that we will have energy and love to give to others and to the world? The answer is: *by loving and giving to ourselves, first.*

There are many ways for us to love and to care for ourselves. The possibilities are infinite. One way to learn to love yourself is to act as if you already do.

You can begin to love yourself by nourishing and caring for your body: eat healthy foods and exercise regularly. Give yourself a special treat like a reflexology session, a facial, a pedicure, or a gym membership. Take some fun breaks because having fun in life is also important.

Another very important way to enhance self-love and self-esteem is to be aware of your self-talk (those things that you say to yourself inside your head). Speak to yourself in ways that are more kind, and less mean or abusive. We are known to be our own worst critics: When we make a mistake, this critical voice inside our head beats up on us, saying things like, "That was so stupid! ... I can't do anything right! ... What a loser!" We need to replace these negative messages with more positive ones. For example, "I made a mistake. That's okay: That is how I learn. I'll know better the next time."

With awareness, over time, you can "catch yourself" when your self-talk is negative change the message to something more positive and "uplifting." Know that the critical inner voice, inside your head, no longer has permission to speak, you are free to speak for yourself and make up your own mind about yourself. Don't just "catch yourself being wrong." "Catch yourself being right."

In other words, don't just catch the voice of your inner critic, without stopping it from beating up on you. When you do something well, or when you find yourself saying the right things to yourself or to others, be sure to reward yourself: acknowledge yourself verbally, give yourself a pat on the back, or treat yourself to something special.

At this point in your life lesson training your master teacher is beginning see promise in you because you are showing signs of falling in love with yourself. Keep doing your assignments.

* Be good to yourself.

* Treat yourself well. Replenish yourself. Upon completing each assignment you will discover that, the more you love yourself, the more you will be able to give love to others - and the more others will want to be around you and give back to you. This is a win-win situation. Loving yourself will ultimately benefit the lives of others you encounter, as well as your own life.

It is by learning the love myself life lesson, that you will be able to manifest your gifts and talents that you are created to share with the world. In reality we are the children of the Universe filled with loving energy which desires that we fulfill our dreams and live each day to its fullest giving thanks.

When we are in full appreciation of ourselves we can respond more compassionately to those who are not. We can recognize the insecurity which lies beneath the words of people who must praise and talk about themselves, to convince themselves that they're worthy through convincing us. Instead of either judging them negatively you can find ways of expressing appreciation for them to who they are, not for what they do. When we recognize that self-love is how we honor ourselves and our inner spirit, through exercising our gifts and talents in generous act of sharing. We also discover that with this perspective we can honor the uniqueness of others and our connection to them.

You can now take your final exam on the love yourself life lesson. Your master teacher wants you to pass, so you are given a study sheet with all the answers needed to pass this course. Learning to honor yourself moves you to the head of the class. Learn to be a master of this lesson and you will be the valedictory of your class.

* Honoring yourself and who you really are. Love is your birthright
  "We are not human beings having a spiritual experience, we are spiritual beings having a human experience." Teilhard de Chardin

* Telling the highest truth, which is we are powerful beings capable of creating joy and success or pain and suffering in our lives? We are not destined to be victims. We have the power to choose, and this power is both the greatest responsibility we have and the greatest opportunity.

* Honoring who you are becoming. Self-love involves recognizing that you are constantly evolving and growing to become a more powerful and more loving being.

* Honoring your feelings and responding to those feelings. Remember, feelings are important signals, and even the so-called negative feelings of anger and fear serve the important purpose of alerting us to the obstacles in our life.

* Release the shackles of the past. Let go of the past, release the pain, and forgive. Forgive means to stop being angry about or resentful against people, problems or situations. It is seeing how we've allowed the past to control us. When we forgive ourselves and let go we can really change and be free to move forward in life,

* Feeling more powerful and able to create the success and happiness we want. The world owes you nothing. You were born deserving the many blessing that the universe has in store for you. Through forgiveness you are able to live your life passion sharing your gifts and talents that will help in heal the universe.

Recognizing that the universe is made of love. Life is a song - sing it.....Life is a game - play it.......Life is a challenge - meet it......Life is a dream - realize it.......Life is a sacrifice - offer it.......Life is love -enjoy it. ~ Sai Baba

The highest esteem in honoring yourself is to have compassion for yourself and for where you are in learning the lesson of life. Remember always that you are a truly loveable person and that you deserve the best kind and loving treatment given to you by you. When you can give this precious gift to yourself, you are truly in love with that wonderful, bold, sexy, beautiful, fearless, confident, courageous woman you are created to be.

We are fast approaching the end of this life lesson journey. Here are the tips I personally used to l fall in love with myself by Louise Hay.

Stop All Criticism. Criticism never changes a thing. Refuse to criticize yourself. Accept yourself exactly as you are. Everybody changes. When you criticize yourself, your changes are negative. When you approve of yourself, your changes are positive.

Don't Scare Yourself. Stop terrorizing yourself with your thoughts. It's a dreadful way to live. Find a mental image that gives you pleasure (mine is yellow roses), and immediately switch your scary thought to a pleasure thought.

Be Gentle And Kind And Patient. Be gentle with yourself. Be kind to yourself. Be patient with yourself as you learn the new ways of thinking. Treat yourself as you would someone you really loved.

Be Kind To Your Mind. Self-hatred is only hating your own thoughts. Don't hate yourself for having the thoughts. Gently change your thoughts.

Praise Yourself. Criticism breaks down the inner spirit. Praise builds it up. Praise yourself as much as you can. Tell yourself how well you are doing with every little thing.

Support Yourself. Find ways to support yourself. Reach out to friends and allow them to help you. It is being strong to ask for help when you need it.

Be Loving To Your Negatives. Acknowledge that you created them to fulfill a need.

Now you are finding new, positive ways to fulfill those needs. So lovingly release the old negative patterns.

Take Care Of Your Body. Learn about nutrition. What kind of fuel does your body need to have optimum energy and vitality? Learn about exercise. What kind of exercise can you enjoy? Cherish and revere the temple you live in.

Mirror Work. Look into your eyes often. Express this growing sense of love you have for yourself. Forgive yourself looking into the mirror. Talk to your parents looking into the mirror. Forgive them too. At least once a day say: "I love you, I really love you!"

LOVE YOURSELF... DO IT NOW. Don't wait until you get well, or lose the weight, or get the new job, or the new relationship. Begin now - and do the best you can.

I honor and acknowledge you. I have shared the life lesson secrets of the empowered woman, I have learned from on how to love yourself unconditionally. Loving yourself unconditionally is what gives you the courage to be yourself. Every successful woman started from the same place you are now. They too wanted a different like experience. To achieve their dreams and passions they enrolled in the life lesson 101 training program. By learning to love yourself is how you create the life of your dreams. When you learn to be clear on what you want, what you are looking for and how to make it happen you join the multitude of empowered women worldwide living the life of your dreams.

Empowerment tip This hidden power is lying dormant inside every woman begging you to use it so you can become the woman you are created to be sharing your power of unconditional love. Congratulations you can join the students of the universe studying the lessons of life as together we grow and evolve into become "*free spirited butterflies*".

Self-love is the foundation of our loving practice. Without it our other efforts to love fail. Giving ourselves love we provide our inner being with the opportunity to have the unconditional love we may have always longed to receive from someone ~ else.bell hooks

Our deepest fear is not that we are inadequate. Our deepest fear is that we are powerful beyond measure. It is our light, not our darkness that frightens us most. We ask ourselves, 'Who am I to be brilliant, gorgeous, talented, and famous?' Actually, who are you not to be? You are a child of God. Your playing small does not serve the world. There is nothing enlightened about shrinking so that people won't feel insecure around you. We were born to make manifest the glory of God that is within us. It's not just in some of us; it's in all of us. And when we let our own light shine, we unconsciously give other people permission to do the same. As we are liberated from our own fear, our presence automatically liberates others ~ From the movie AKEELAH and the BEE

Are You A Self Proclaimed Woman?

When I stand up for myself and my beliefs, they call me a bitch.

When I stand up for those I love, they call me a bitch.

When I speak my mind, think my own thoughts or do things my own way, they call me a bitch.......

BITCHOLOGY

* Being a bitch means I won't compromise what's in my heart.

* It means I live my life MY way.

* It means I won't allow anyone to step on me

When I refuse to tolerate injustice and speak against it, I am defined as a bitch......
The same thing happens when I take time for myself instead of being everyone's maid, or When I act a little selfish.......
It means I have the courage and strength to allow myself to be who I truly am and won't become anyone else's idea of what they think I 'should' be......
I am outspoken, opinionated and determined. I want what I want and there is nothing wrong with that........ So try to stomp on me, try to douse my inner flame, try to squash every ounce of beauty I hold within me........ You won't succeed.

And if that makes me a bitch, so be it. I embrace the title and am proud to bear it.

B - Babe	**B** = Bold	**B** = Beautiful
I - In	**I** = Intelligent	**I** = Individual
T - Total	**T** = Talented	**T** = That
C - Control of	**C** = Charming	**C** = Can
H – Herself	**H** = Hell of a Woman	**H** = Handle anything

ABCs of Loving Yourself by Dani www.positivelypresent.com

Accept your body...... Sure, there are things you can change about your body, but, for the most part, you've got to work with what you've got. Remember: you are who you are. You should love yourself no matter what shape or size you are. You are awesome. You are beautiful. You are YOU. Don't ever forget that!

Be who you are........ You are not your body. The essence of you comes from within -- from your mind, your personality, your heart. I often find it hard to remember that I am not what I look like, but, when I remind myself of this, I realize there is so much more to me than appearance.

Cultivate a health environment..... Put yourself in a healthier place. Keeping fresh fruits and veggies around, eating healthy and exercising are great ways to love your body (and yourself!). And don't forget to take care of your mental health. Consider meditation to get your mind in a calmer, happier place.

Dive into self love...... Okay, so you're having trouble loving yourself. You look in the mirror and think, "YUCK!" Try looking into self-help books or blogs that encourage positive thinking about life and, more specifically, about body image. Sometimes reading up on loving yourself can really help you put it into action.

Embrace your abilities...... Think about what you do well. Your body is only a part of who you are. You might be a great writer, a great athlete, an amazing parent. No matter what you are, there is more to you than your appearance. Embrace what you're good at and spend more time indulging in these activities.

Forget about comparisons......Stop comparing yourself to others. No matter what you do, you probably will not ever look like Halle Berry or Sandra Bullock. But that's okay! You are beautiful in your own way and you will always and forever be you. Accept yourself, love yourself, and stop looking to others to see what you "should" look like.

137

Get moving..... I don't know about you, but when I get in a not-loving-myself funk, I don't want to do anything. I just want to lay around and think about how pathetic it is that I'm not doing anything by laying around. Break the cycle. Get off the couch and use that awesome body and mind!

Have Hope...... Even if you're struggling with self-love, don't give up hope. It might be hard right now, but the more effort and time you put into it, the more you will learn to love yourself. Hope is crucial when it comes to learning to love yourself. Believe in your own ability to achieve self-love.

Indulge in what you love..... Every so often let yourself eat or do whatever you wouldn't normally. I'm sure you've read this a million times, but if you completely cut yourself off from something, you're more likely to go nuts the next time it comes along so let yourself indulge every once and awhile.

Join something fun...... Joining a group (or even starting a blog, which feels like joining something) can really help you with your image of yourself. Meet new people. Try new things. Being happy in general can make you happier with how you look so check out some groups you can join.

Keep thinking positively....... Ah, my favorite! Keep thinking positively -- no matter what. So you gained 5 pounds. So you got a terrible haircut. So what. Keep thinking positively! No matter how bad you feel about yourself, there is always something good. Focus on the good, the positive, and push the negative from your mind.

Let go of your past....... You were a size two in high school. Sure, that's super, but you're not in high school anymore. Remind yourself that this is where you are now. You may have been something else in the past -- thinner, prettier, more muscular – but here you are now. In the present. Love who you are right now.

Motivate yourself...... You are the best motivational tool you have. Other people might encourage you, but only YOU can really motivate yourself. Do whatever you have to remind yourself how great you are. Read books. Get off the couch. Talk to friends. Do whatever you have to motivate your inner desire for self love.

Never say never........ You're looking in the mirror moaning, "I will never lose this weight." You know what? You're right. With that attitude, you won't make any changes at all. You'll settle, thinking there's no hope, and you'll be unhappy. If you believe you can change something, you can. Never say never.

Open up to new ideas...... Try something different. If you're not in love with your look, try something new. New clothes. New makeup. New workout routine. Experimenting with new things isn't going to solve your body image issues (that comes from within),but you can give yourself a little boost by trying out something new.

Put on your best outfit...... For those of you who read the post "rainy days and Mondays..." you know that sometimes just a change of clothes can change your perspective. Don't stay in sweatpants all day. Don't settle for average or blah or you will feel average and blah. Dress up. Put in the effort and you'll feel a lot better about yourself.

Question your perception...... You look in the mirror. You see ugly, fat, tired. But is that what's really there? As I talked about in my last post, your mind can really distort your thoughts. Sometimes what we see isn't what's really there. Keep the positive thoughts in the forefront. Avoid looking for the bad and try to keep a positive outlook.

Remember what you love...... You hate your stomach, but your love your eyes. You hate your arms, but you love your thighs. Focus on the good parts of you. We often spend so much time obsessing about what we don't like about ourselves that we forget to spend time thinking about what we do love. Make a list of your favorite parts of you (including those that aren't physical!).

Stop judging...... You are your worst critic. You are judging yourself much, much more harshly than anyone around you is. Stop it. Stop it right now. There is absolutely no good reason to critique yourself in a harsh or demeaning manner. Love yourself first and the world will love you too.

Take time for you....... Your body is the only one you have. Take time to pamper yourself. Do whatever, you have to do to get some quality alone time. Take a bath. Take a walk. Take a vacation. Whatever you do, take some time to be alone with yourself, to rejuvenate your body and your mind.

Understand your needs...... What do you really need? What makes your body happy? When you exercise and eat healthy foods, does your body feel better? When you get plenty of rest, do you wake up refreshed? Think about what your body asks for and give it what it needs. The better your body feels, the better you will feel about it.

Vacate your mind..... Take time to do a mental cleaning throwing away unused, unwanted and out dated thoughts and memories. Open the window of your mind to fresh ideas so you are no longer a prisoner in your own mind. Release your mental obsessions about your looks and appearance that is to the point of being unhealthy. If you're doing this, stop. Get out of your mind and free yourself.

Watch what you say...... Are you always saying to your friends, "Ugh, I look terrible." or "This makes me look fat?"? If so, think about what you're saying. The more negative things you say about yourself, the more you will start to really believe what you're saying (and others might too). Try, just once, saying, "Wow, I look great!"

X-ray your desires...... Think about -- I mean, really think about -- why you want that piece of chocolate cake or that new handbag. Will external things make you feel better? You bet! But the feel-good feelings are only temporary. Lasting happiness comes from within so give some thought to what you really want.

Yank yourself out of a routine...... Routines can be deadly. They set us in patterns that feel old and tired, that make us feel as if we are old and tired. Some routines are good and
necessary, but what routines do you have in your life that aren't good? What can you do to change them, to make them more positive experiences?

Zap any negative thoughts....... Last but certainly not least! Getting rid of negative thoughts about yourself and your body is one of the most important things you can do for yourself.
Whatever you need to do to do this, do it. Read books. Go on a retreat. Get rid of negative people in your life. Whatever you do, be positive about.

THE BEAUTY OF AN EMPOWERED WOMAN

The beauty of a woman is not in the clothes she wears,

The figure she carries, or the way she combs her hair.

The beauty of a woman must be seen from her eyes,

Because that is the doorway to her heart,

The place where love resides.

The beauty of a woman is not in a facial mole,

But true beauty in a woman is reflected in her soul.

It is the caring that she lovingly gives,

The passion that she shows.

The beauty of a woman

With passing years -- only grows.

A TRIBUTE TO THE EMPOWERED WOMAN

ONLY A WOMAN
Can work full time while finishing school, raising respectful and intelligent children, be active in the PTA, be the pastor's secretary, and the choir president and a make it all seem effortless

ONLY A WOMAN
Can make a $1.00 out of 15 Cents

ONLY A WOMAN
Can go from the boardroom to the 'hood and "keep it real" in both places.

ONLY A WOMAN
Can slap the taste out of your mouth.

ONLY A WOMAN
Can put a man and his mistress/girlfriend on pins and needles just by walking into the room.

ONLY A WOMAN
Can live below poverty level and yet set fashion trends.

ONLY A WOMAN
Can fight two struggles everyday and make it look easy.

ONLY A WOMAN
Can make a child happy on Christmas Day even if he didn't get a darn thing.

ONLY A WOMAN
Can be admired and fantasized about by men of all cultures and income and know that when she makes her selection it's done out of sincerity, and not a political or economic move

ONLY A WOMAN
Can be 75 years old and look 45!

ONLY A WOMAN
Can be the mother of civilization.

———

I am my own woman~ Evita Perón

Take Action!!!

You have been given two great gifts your mind and your time. It is up to you to do whatever you please with both. With each life experience you face, you and only you have the power to accept the situation and do nothing about it or you can make a lifestyle change that will give you a better quality of life. Every day you can decide how you want to live your life. It can be to live a life filled with hatred, anger, lack and sadness or love, peace, abundance and happiness. The choice is yours and only yours

Choose to share this knowledge with the women in your life and choose to be there for them as they too learn their life lesson. Life lessons are a gift from the Universe to be shared freely as we learn and grow into becoming empowered women. To be an empowered woman is to give back to the Universe the gift of *Love and Thankfulness*. This is the gift of *Life* that the Universe freely gives to you.

You and the women of the world who are learning the lesson of life are planting the seeds for your daughters and their daughters that will make a difference for generations to come.

I wish you health, prosperity, abundance, love, peace and happiness with this fabulous gift called life.

Njideka N. Olatunde
Your Evolving Free Spirited Butterfly

One is not born a woman, one becomes one ~ Simone de Beauvoir

Resource Section

The Feminate Factor Edumercial

There is nothing new under the sun only recycled experiences and lessons ~ Njideka N. Olatunde

The Feminate Factor™.com is the go-to destination, for any woman who aspires to take back control of her life and let the little girl inside come out and plays!

What Is The Feminate Factor™ Mentoring Program?
It is a three phase program created to teach women how to get fired up about life so they can be fabulously successful, blissfully happy, and lovin' it. The Feminate Factor was created as a leading provider of "how-to" information designed to inspire and empower women on "How to Say NO to Disappointment, Fear, Rejection and Pain by saying YES to Living a Happy and Fun Filled Life..... Like the "*Free Spirited Butterfly*"™

How does The Feminate Factor™ Mentoring Program work?
It empowers women to feel good about who they are, where they are right now in their life using *The Evolving Butterfly Effect*™ modeling the development stages of the butterfly.

The Feminate Factor Mentoring Program®

Step One: Beginners - Cocoon Phase
Program Title: **How to Be Happy In an Unhappy World**
A Self Help Guide on How to Reconnect with Who You Really Are

Step Two: Intermediate Caterpillar Phase
Program Title: **Staging A Come Back**
A Complete Program for Women Tired of Putting Their Dreams on the Back Burner and are Ready to Do Their Own Thing

Step Three: Advance: Evolving Butterfly Phase
Program Title: **The Art of Being A Woman**
A Step by Step System on how to be a Brand New Woman with Authentic Power

What Are the Program Benefits?
What if, You could wake up every morning to a day full of spectacular success, fulfillment, passion and joy (*Self confidence*)
How about in your job or career, knocking the socks off, your competition or being recognized as a valuable asset, or getting the job or results you really want. (*Career*)
Just imagine what it feels like to never say "I can't afford to buy what I want or live where I want" (*Financial*)
How about having more time in your life to play and have fun with your children or just enjoy life doing whatever you want to do whenever you want to do it. (*Time*)

These and many more benefits are in store for you with The Feminate Factor Mentoring Program. The ultimate benefit is to build self-esteem and confidence by empowering women to take back control of their lives, make lifestyle changes that turns stress to calmness with the desired results being a new and improved woman who is powerful, self confident, bold, beautiful and living her passion like the "*Free Spirited Butterfly*"™.

Life Style Reality Check

It's Not What You Look Like....It's Who You Really Are
We All Have Dreams and Desires For Our Lives.
Are You the Woman You Always Wanted To Be?
Do you find yourself stressed out, overwhelmed, and increasingly unhappy?
Are financial issues worrying you and you don't know what to do?
Do you feel unmotivated and uninspired with your personal and professional life?
Are you working hard and you're not getting the recognition or compensation you deserve?
Do you have a burning desire to be successful, healthy, financially free and happy?
The biggest adventure you can ever take to pursue your dreams is living the life of a "*Free Spirited Butterflies*"™.

Your reality check question: How much more of your life are you going to spend letting time steal your dreams? You have lost many years and will continue to loose more years if you don't enroll in the **Feminate Factor Mentoring Program®**.

Your life is made up of time and how you spend your time ~ Heatherr Jumah

Register Now at www.thefeminatefactor.com

TheFeminate Factor®

F emales **E** njoying **M** ore **I** nner **N** atural **A** wareness **T** hat's **E** ternal (because of) **F** aith **A** nd **C** ourage **T** o **O** btain **R** esults

Njideka Olatunde, founder and CEO of Be Empowered, LLC. I am affectionately known as the "*Free Spirited Butterfly*"™ and creator of The Feminate Factor Educational System®. It is my desire and passion to help women create and live the lives of their dreams. My life purpose is to inspire and empower women to change their lives by developing self belief, self confidence, and successful skills needed to live passionate, prosperous, and powerful lives.

Njideka is a Teacher of Universal Life Lessons, a mentor and consultant specializing in working with women at a cross road in their lives seeking to find a meaning and purpose for the life they are living. She is on a mission to empower women worldwide to use their hidden feminate power to restore happiness once again in their life. She is dedicated to showing women how to avoid emotional and physical pain, how to improve the quality of life and to become a strong independent, successful and confident women. She is the expert women turn to when they are ready to take back control of their lives and let the world know they are a new woman with a brand new attitude.

Njideka encourages women using *The Evolving Butterfly Effect*™ to "take back control of their lives" and she is introducing the system to women around the world through her multi-media company The Feminate Factor Media Network. She believes the time is now for women to learn how to feel good about themselves and begin to live the life they truly want. The reason that Njideka knows the importance of making lifestyle changes is because she has her own Evolving Butterfly Effect™ story to share. She has many stories to share on surviving the many ups, downs, highs and lows on the emotional roller coaster I called Life.

She has made money and lost money. She has lived in prosperity and I has lived in poverty. She has held professional and management positions and I has held low skilled labor jobs. She has had wonderful nurturing relationships and I has had negative abusive relationships. She has experienced the best of health and I has experienced some serious health issues. She has been a single parent dealing with all the things that go along with it. Let's not talk about the family and how they can be a contributor on your roller coaster ride. As you can see whatever you maybe facing right now trust me, Njideka can relate.

Njideka has consulted with women in making lifestyle changes across the United States, Caribbean, China and Africa through her seminars, Teleclass and consulting practice working with hundreds of clients over the years. Based on her years of experience formally and informally mentoring women, she understands that the key to success begins in your mind. She believes that every woman who is dedicated and committed to developing a success mindset and success skills can create and live the life of her dreams. She also understands that women have unique challenges they must confront and overcome, if they are to create amazing lives, she believes that until you overcome limiting beliefs, have the courage to face your fears and confront obstacles, possess resilience with unwavering commitment and a willingness to take "risks" it is unlikely you will live the life you desire.

Njideka can actually relate to your situations. She knows your struggles in trying to change and overcome when everything in your world is falling to pieces and there is no one you can go to who understands. It is for this reason The Feminate Factor Educational System® was created to be a support base and network designed to assist women in developing the skills necessary to overcome self limiting beliefs, develop self confidence, rediscover their courage and reawaken their passion to live powerful, successful and happy lives. Whatever dreams you have for your life, Njideka encourages you to pursue those dreams and passions that live in your heart so you can live your own version of the *"Free Spirited Butterfly Lifestyle"* ... a life of fun, happiness, success, prosperity passion, freedom and adventure!

The future belongs to those who believe in the beauty of their Dreams ~ Eleanor Roosevelt

CPSIA information can be obtained at www.ICGtesting.com
Printed in the USA
BVOW021140270812

298911BV00016B/265/P